ASIA PACIFIC SECURITY OUTLOOK 2000

The cosponsors of this project wish to thank

Asia Pacific Agenda Project

The Nippon Foundation

ASIA PACIFIC
SECURITY OUTLOOK
2000

edited by
Richard W. Baker
and
Charles E. Morrison

cosponsored by

 ASEAN Institutes for Strategic
and International Studies

 East-West
Center

Japan Center for
International Exchange

AN APAP PROJECT

Tokyo • Japan Center for International Exchange • *New York*

Copyediting by Elmer Luke and Pamela J. Noda.
Cover and typographic design by Becky Davis, EDS Inc.,
Editorial & Design Services. Typesetting and production by EDS Inc.

Printed in Japan.
ISBN 4-88907-039-7

Distributed worldwide outside Japan by Brookings Institution Press,
1775 Massachusetts Avenue, N.W., Washington, D.C. 20036-2188 U.S.A.

Japan Center for International Exchange
9-17 Minami Azabu 4-chome, Minato-ku, Tokyo 106-0047 Japan

URL: http://www.jcie.or.jp

Japan Center for International Exchange, Inc. (JCIE/USA)
1251 Avenue of the Americas, New York, N.Y. 10020 U.S.A.

Contents

Foreword

This is the fourth in the annual *Asia Pacific Security Outlook* series, sponsored by the ASEAN Institutes for Strategic and International Studies, the East-West Center, and the Japan Center for International Exchange (JCIE).

The *Outlook* does not seek to develop a consensus view of regional security trends and issues. Rather, it presents the distinctive national perspectives of most member countries of the ASEAN Regional Forum (ARF), in a form that facilitates comparison and the identification of areas where perceptions or interests differ. The objective is both to increase mutual understanding within the community of security analysts in the region and to help elucidate the key issues that will affect future regional security and stability.

Participants in the project are drawn from academic and research institutions in the member countries, not from the government bureaucracies. Thus, the views expressed in the background papers and in the country chapters based on those papers do not necessarily represent government views. However, the chapters attempt to present the mainstream points of view in the government and society of each country, as well as to indicate the areas in which there are uncertainties, differences, or policy debates.

The *Outlook* has not yet achieved the objective of covering all ARF member countries. However, this edition of the *Outlook* has again expanded, to include for the first time chapters on Brunei Darussalam and Cambodia.

We wish to express our appreciation to all those who contributed to *Outlook 2000*. The analysts and paper authors contributed their considerable expertise and substantial time to the project. Nishihara

Masashi is a codirector of the *Outlook* project, along with Charles E. Morrison and Jusuf Wanandi. Richard W. Baker of the East-West Center again undertook much of the editing of this volume, as well as provided the background paper on the United States. Wada Shūichi of JCIE again coordinated the activities associated with the project, including its November 1999 workshop in Tokyo, and Pamela J. Noda, also of JCIE, again oversaw the copyediting and publication process.

The organizing institutions are grateful to the Nippon Foundation for its continuing financial support of the *Asia Pacific Security Outlook* as a part of the larger Asia Pacific Agenda Project, a multifaceted activity designed to promote policy-oriented intellectual dialogue among nongovernmental analysts in the Asia Pacific region.

CHARLES E. MORRISON
PRESIDENT
EAST-WEST CENTER

JUSUF WANANDI
FOUNDING MEMBER
ASEAN INSTITUTES FOR
STRATEGIC AND INTERNATIONAL STUDIES

YAMAMOTO TADASHI
PRESIDENT
JAPAN CENTER FOR INTERNATIONAL EXCHANGE

Regional Overview

As Asia Pacific enters a new millennium, the basic features of post–cold war security relations remain. No country is in open conflict with another, and positive economic and human interaction is increasing across even the most volatile of large power relationships. Of the countries most affected by the 1997–1998 Asian economic crisis, most are recovering rapidly. Cooperation among nations continues to progress. There is ample reason for optimism about the future of security relations in the region.

Nevertheless, there are signs that stability in Asia Pacific is fragile, and in many ways the outlook appears more uncertain than at any time in the past decade. These signs include the growing difficulties in large power relationships, particularly as regards China and the United States, and the acquisition of sophisticated weaponry associated with potential conflict in the Taiwan Strait and the Korean peninsula. The region remains heavily armed. (For an overview of defense spending in Asia Pacific and armed forces strength in the region, see table 1.) At the domestic level, the processes of nation building remain incomplete. This was starkly demonstrated by Indonesia, which failed in its twenty-five-year effort to integrate East Timor into the nation and which is now challenged by revitalized separatist movements and ethnic tensions. In few countries in Asia Pacific can the domestic political order be said to be firmly in place.

The combination of international and domestic stresses does not necessarily point to any immediate danger for the region. But it does suggest uncertainty and the potential for a deteriorating security environment. In particular, the 1999 crisis in East Timor illustrates that smoldering tensions, at least at the local level, can quickly ignite into flames.

Table 1. Asia Pacific Defense Spending and Armed Forces (1998)

Country	Defense Spending[a]					Armed Forces[b]					
	US$ m.	% GDP	Rank	GDP (US$)	Rank	Number	Rank	% Pop.	Rank	Pop. (000s)	Rank
United States	270,200	3.2	8	8,500,000	1	1,371,500	3	.50	8	273,133	4
Europe (EU/NATO)[c]	166,542	2.2	12	7,737,000	2	1,684,068	2	.48	10	353,576	3
Russia	55,000	5.0	4	1,100,000	4	1,004,100	6	.69	6	146,300	6
Japan	37,700	1.0	19	3,800,000	3	236,300	11	.19	16	126,515	7
China[d]	37,500	5.3	3	703,000	5	2,480,000	1	.20	15	1,244,000	1
India	14,100	3.0	10	469,000	7	1,173,000	4	.12	19	999,839	2
South Korea	13,200	3.1	9	426,000	8	672,000	7	1.43	4	47,000	11
Australia	8,100	2.1	13	390,000	9	55,200	17	.29	12	19,082	15
Canada	6,800	1.1	18	604,000	6	60,600	16	.21	14	29,236	12
Indonesia	5,000	2.6	11	189,000	10	298,000	10	.15	17	203,479	5
Singapore	4,800	5.0	5	96,000	12	73,000	15	2.28	2	3,200	19
Thailand	2,100	1.5	15	137,000	11	306,000	9	.48	9	63,726	10
Malaysia	1,500	1.7	14	88,000	13	105,000	14	.48	11	22,094	13
North Korea	1,300	9.3	1	14,000	17	1,082,000	5	5.03	1	21,500	14
Philippines	1,000	1.5	16	65,000	14	110,000	13	.15	18	75,659	9
Vietnam	925	3.4	7	27,000	16	484,000	8	.60	7	80,433	8
New Zealand	881	1.5	17	58,000	15	9,530	19	.25	13	3,835	18
Brunei	378	6.9	2	5,500	18	5,000	18	1.54	3	325	20
Cambodia	152	4.2	6	3,600	20	149,000	12	1.40	5	10,654	16
Papua New Guinea	56	1.0	20	5,500	19	4,300	20	.09	20	4,759	17

SOURCE: Based on data from *Military Balance 1999/2000*. London: International Institute for Strategic Studies (IISS), 1999.

[a]Defense spending figures are IISS estimates of total defense spending (not official budgets).

[b]Figures are for active duty regular armed forces.

[c]Europe figures are for the twelve members of the European Union that are also members of the North Atlantic Treaty Organization: Belgium, Denmark, France, Germany, Greece, Italy, Luxembourg, the Netherlands, Norway, Portugal, Spain, and the United Kingdom.

[d]GDP and defense spending estimates for China are based on purchasing power parity, including extra-budgetary military spending (China's official 1998 defense budget was US$11.0 billion).

Assumptions Challenged

The first post–cold war decade was met with a generally positive assessment of the international security environment. This optimism was based on a number of widely—albeit not universally—held assumptions that are increasingly coming under question today. These include:

- The assumption that security guarantees and the forward military presence of the United States are benign and stabilizing. This notion had wide currency in countries traditionally associated with the Western alliance. However, intervention in Kosovo by the North Atlantic Treaty Organization (NATO)—accompanied by perceptions of a growing U.S. military superiority—has led to questions about the use, or potential use, of American power in a region where principles of sovereignty and noninterference in internal affairs have high standing.
- The assumption that economics are in command. As regards the developing nations of Asia, the prevailing belief was that economic modernization was of such priority that countries would defer difficult political issues that might undermine the economy. Periodic crises in the Korean peninsula and the Taiwan Strait reoccur, however, despite the economic benefits of increased transactions and nonbelligerent behavior.
- The assumption that the current legal and political status of Taiwan could be maintained over the longer term without resort to force or serious threat thereof. Challenges to the status quo seem to arise with increasing frequency, usually driven by domestic political imperatives.
- The assumption that substantial regional arms procurements have more to do with modernization and new missions than with competitive tensions, a view set forward in previous volumes of the *Asia Pacific Security Outlook*. Some arms acquisition and deployment, however, particularly in the Taiwan Strait, have features of a classic arms race, in which each side seeks to alter the balance of military power in its favor.
- The assumption that, for major countries of the region, the processes of basic nation building have been completed. The ethnic, religious, and separatist strife in Indonesia suggest otherwise for one centrally important country.
- The assumption that Japan's defense posture is essentially pacifistic and status quo–oriented. This idea is being challenged by some who

believe Japan is rapidly moving toward a new, more assertive security posture, whether in cooperation with or separate from the United States.

• The assumption that regional cooperation on the part of the Association of Southeast Asian Nations (ASEAN) would build stronger relations among the countries of Southeast Asia. Today, ASEAN does not appear to be providing the sense of order and security that it once did—owing to such factors as expansion of ASEAN's membership to include a more diverse group of countries and leadership concerns in several members.

Some of these assumptions may still prove valid. But the simultaneous challenging of so many basic assumptions about the underpinnings of regional stability suggests that Asia Pacific may be at a critical juncture. The test will be whether the region can devise a more durable framework for the future.

WATCH LIST ISSUES

In its initial edition in 1997, the *Asia Pacific Security Outlook* identified four watch list issues: the Korean peninsula, large power relations, arms acquisitions, and territorial disputes. These issues were considered manageable but of such importance that they should be carefully monitored.

Security analysts associated with the *Asia Pacific Security Outlook 2000* generally see little change concerning Korea and the territorial issues, but identified worrisome signs in large power relations and weapons procurement. The situation on the Korean peninsula continues to be volatile; there were tensions in mid-1999 over North Korea's challenge to the Northern Limit Line in the West Sea (Yellow Sea) and its threat to test a second Taepodong missile. A U.S.–North Korean agreement, however, was successful in deferring the missile test, and the Perry Report, by former U.S. Defense Secretary William Perry, articulated the basis for a U.S.–Japanese–South Korean policy which sought to constrain North Korea's nuclear weapons and missile programs in return for more open economic ties. Toward the end of 1999, the hitherto frosty Japan–North Korean relationship improved, and the security situation on the Korean peninsula slipped into the twenty-first century looking more encouraging than it has for some time.

However, the progress of inter-Korean relations has been anything but linear, and the basic security dilemma for North Korea remains, and even intensifies, as its relative economic and military position continues to deteriorate. This has spurred the search for weapons of mass destruction to rectify the balance or, at least, to serve as a bargaining tool.

Similarly, there was little apparent change in the various territorial disputes in the region. Northeast Asia was quiescent in 1999. In the South China Sea, the Philippines protested activity by China and Malaysia on reefs that it regarded as being in Philippine territorial waters. But the year saw no change in the territorial status quo, no clashes, and no breakthroughs on the diplomatic front that would help to resolve disputes. Thus, territory remains an irritant in key bilateral relationships as well as an obstacle to regional security cooperation.

The worrisome trends among large power relations center on China's relations with the United States. Despite intensive economic Sino-American interaction, the political relationship has continued to be volatile. In 1997–1998, an exchange of visits by leaders placed the relationship on an upward course, and this was reflected in a more positive Asia Pacific security outlook. But in 1999, there was a sharp reversal following the NATO campaign in Kosovo in March, which China opposed, the U.S. rejection of an impressive trade offer by Premier Zhu Rongji during a Washington visit in April, and the U.S. bombing of the Chinese embassy in Belgrade, followed by Chinese demonstrations at U.S. embassy offices in China. The tone of the relationship improved in the latter part of the year after a meeting between presidents Bill Clinton and Jiang Zemin at the September leaders' meeting in Auckland of the Asia-Pacific Economic Cooperation (APEC) forum. The embassy bombing was quietly put to the side, and a trade agreement was reached later in the year under which the United States would support China's entry into the World Trade Organization. Despite this recovery, however, events in the Sino-American relationship during the year reveal the deep suspicions underlying this relationship. Domestic politics increasingly complicate the management of relations in both capitals.

Two sensitive issues pose particular challenges to the United States and China: the status of Taiwan, and questions of human rights and humanitarian intervention. The Taiwan issue has grown more difficult in recent years owing to politics in both Taiwan and the mainland. Analysts associated with the *Asia Pacific Security Outlook 2000* rated Taiwan leader Lee Teng-hui's statement that relations between Taiwan and China should be on a "state-to-state" basis as the single most negative security development during 1999. Analysts were also concerned about weapons deployment in the region, noting China's recent missile deployment across from Taiwan. The Chinese regard this as a response to a more provocative posturing by Taiwan, and Taiwanese weapons modernization, but this response in turn increases incentive for Taiwan to move forward in seeking a missile defense system from the United States. Thus, forces are in place for a classic arms race—a competitive weapons buildup accompanied by higher-pitched rhetoric and an increased threat to use the weapons.

The question of humanitarian intervention, given new visibility by Kosovo and East Timor in the same year, also figured large in relations between China and the United States as well as between Russia and the United States. Many governments in Asia have stressed the principles of sovereignty and noninterference in internal affairs. What was especially disturbing then was that intervention in Yugoslavia was initiated by NATO acting on its own, with concurrence by the UN Security Council. The East Timor intervention, on the other hand, coming only after agreement by Indonesia to outside forces and endorsement by the United Nations, was legitimate. Issues surrounding humanitarian intervention, which for China and Russia have special importance arising from Western cries of human rights abuses in such sensitive regions as Tibet, Xinjiang, and Chechnya, will continue to be the subject of discussion and debate among Asia Pacific nations.

Adding to these tensions is the perception of a growing military power gap between the United States and other countries due to U.S. superiority in high-technology systems, its economic strength, and the sheer magnitude of its continuing investment in the military (see table 1). Some governments believe that the United States may be more willing to use its military power since its human costs in both the Persian Gulf War and the Kosovo intervention were minimal.

The perception that the world has become more unipolar is very problematic for governments such as China and Russia, which would like to see more multipolarity. Whether this perception continues, and whether it will be shared by other nations over time, will be a major factor affecting future regional and global security trends.

INDONESIA

In Asia Pacific, the country with the most challenging, immediate security problem is Indonesia. The problem is domestic, the result of an implosion of the body politic triggered by the economic crisis rather than any foreign threat. As pointed out in the overview of *Asia Pacific Security Outlook 1999*, Indonesia needs "to rebuild its political system in addition to its economy." During the past year, Indonesia has made substantial progress in developing a new political order. The country carried out its first democratic election in many years without violence, and witnessed the creation of a new government under Abdurrahman Wahid that represented all major political factions.

Despite his physical disabilities and frailties, Wahid is an energetic leader. The challenges he faces, however, are daunting. One is to repair the internal and external damage done by the military's support for pro-Indonesian militia in East Timor, which nearly destroyed the country following its vote for independence. A second, not unrelated challenge for Indonesia is to develop a solid, durable framework for continued democratic and civilian-led government. Third, the country faces a serious separatist challenge in Aceh province and, to a lesser extent, elsewhere. Fourth, ethnic and communal violence in eastern Indonesia continues. Finally, President Wahid leads the one developing Asian country that shows the least signs of recovering from the region's economic crisis.

As a country of more than 200 million people, spanning the strategic links between the Indian Ocean and the South China Sea, and as the linchpin of ASEAN, Indonesia is itself important to the security of Asia Pacific. The difficulties Indonesia faces have significance in that they illustrate the continuing need in emerging Asian nations to build a strong sense of national unity and a durable, widely accepted political order.

POSITIVE ELEMENTS: THE ECONOMIC RECOVERY AND REGIONAL COOPERATION

Aside from the improvement on the Korean peninsula at the end of 1999, two other positive elements in the security outlook are noteworthy as the region enters the twenty-first century: the recovery from economic crisis and a more realistic understanding of the promise of regional cooperation.

ECONOMIC RECOVERY As Asia moves rapidly out of the crisis, there appears to be a greater understanding of the unique features of the crisis as it affected different economies. In South Korea, Malaysia, the Philippines, and Thailand, the recovery has assumed a distinct V-shaped appearance, particularly in South Korea where 10 percent economic growth was achieved in 1999. The Korean economic recovery has been buoyed by the continued strong growth in the United States and a high Japanese yen rate, enabling Korean manufacturers to compete effectively against Japanese rivals. In Thailand and Malaysia, 5 percent growth has positioned the economies in line to achieve precrisis output levels in the year 2000, although Thailand is lagging in restructuring bad loans.

Although dramatic, particularly in comparison with the decade-long Latin American debt crisis of the 1980s, the Asian economic recovery remains tentative in some respects. Ironically, recovery may undermine the political support for corporate and governmental reforms still needed for the longer term. Moreover, three big questions involve the future of the economies of the United States, China, and Japan. The United States continues to enjoy remarkable overall growth with strong productivity growth and relatively stable prices. In China, deflation and debt-burdened banks pose a significant problem, and the growth rate has gradually declined. Nevertheless, discussion of or concern about a Chinese yuan devaluation, regarded as a major threat to the region in 1998, has almost entirely disappeared. In Japan, despite some promising signs and considerable corporate restructuring, economic recovery remains elusive.

Even with these uncertainties and with the significant exception of the ongoing economic-*cum*-political crisis in Indonesia, the countries most affected by the 1997–1998 economic crisis have emerged with few domestic political or security side effects. The economic impact of the crisis was severe, especially for the poor, but the crisis may also have been a needed wake-up call. If sustained, the recovery should provide a basis for enhanced regional cooperation.

REGIONAL COOPERATION   Asia Pacific has long been distinguished by its relative paucity of regional institutions compared to other geographical regions. This began to change in the late 1980s and 1990s with the establishment of dialogue mechanisms for both economic issues—APEC—and political security issues—the ASEAN Regional Forum (ARF). After rising expectations in the mid-1990s, disillusionment set in as APEC proved a weak vehicle for addressing issues associated with the Asian financial crisis, and as its 1998 leaders' meeting failed to agree on a package of trade liberalization measures. In 1999, however, APEC appeared to be making a modest recovery. Its Auckland ministerial and leaders' meetings took place in an atmosphere of down-scaled expectations. APEC's reputation was also enhanced by the increased media attention to the value of "side meetings" that took place before the APEC leaders' meetings, such as the side meeting between presidents Jiang and Clinton and the special ministerial meeting devoted to East Timor.

The ARF process has continued to move ahead, less hindered by overexpectations. There is widespread recognition that in the event of a crisis there is little ARF can do, as was the case with East Timor in 1999. ARF's efforts to move ahead into new areas of cooperation, such as conflict prevention, also remain controversial. ARF does, however, enhance contact among governmental security specialists and help build consensus, beginning with the least contentious issues. While its importance should not be overrated, it should also not be discounted.

Another positive sign in the regional picture is "minilateralism"—that is, the growing cooperation among small groups of like-minded countries. Japan, South Korea, and the United States have increased cooperation concerning North Korea. China, Japan, and South Korea have agreed to support research and analysis on economic issues in Northeast Asia. There are increased venues for Northeast Asian–Southeast Asian dialogue, deriving from the cooperation within the Asian component of the Asia-Europe Meeting (ASEM). The Auckland APEC meetings, which occurred just after the East Timor crisis came to a head, were an opportunity for foreign ministers to convene a special and effective meeting on the issue. All these are signs of a growing network of cooperation among small groups that may facilitate conflict avoidance.

STRATEGIC DIALOGUE

That Asia Pacific is undergoing rapid social, economic, and political change is obvious. Some of these changes, such as the increasing economic interdependence and the decline of ideological divides, facilitate the establishment of networks across the lines and provide opportunities for dialogue. An awareness of shared interests can be thus strengthened, and misunderstandings reduced. But other changes in Asia Pacific have increased social tensions and heightened insecurity. Moreover, increasing pluralism complicates foreign policy making at the national level and thus government-to-government international relations.

These changes make critically important the development of a widely understood and accepted framework for managing regional tensions. Asia Pacific is at a crossroads where older institutions are being challenged but consensus is meager on how to strengthen, alter, or replace them. Strategic dialogue among leaders and specialists on the issues—and the principles that govern their resolution—is of central importance to the future security outlook.

ASIA PACIFIC SECURITY OUTLOOK 2000

1 Australia

Australia entered the year 2000 with increased uncertainty in its security outlook and questions about some of the assumptions that have underpinned its security policies in recent years. The economic and political upheaval in Indonesia and the turmoil in East Timor have posed the most significant security challenges for Australia since the Vietnam War. The East Timor crisis highlighted the basic fragility of Indonesia and reinforced both the importance and the limitations of Australia's alliances. Although the Australian government felt obliged to play a leading role in resolving the crisis and is satisfied with its handling of the situation, it has paid a significant price in terms of strained relations with Indonesia. Doubts have also been expressed in other Asian countries about Australia's motives and methods.

The full impact of the East Timor crisis is not yet clear and depends greatly on future developments in Southeast Asia that are beyond Australia's control. However, the experience suggests the need for some reexamination of how Australia's own security relates to that of the wider region, in order to establish how Australia can work more effectively with its neighbors in enhancing stability, and what kind of defense force it will need for this purpose.

Some broader issues in Australia's defense policy, unrelated to changes in regional circumstances, were also thrown into relief by East Timor. Questions have been asked about the level of Australia's defense resources, which had been held under 2 percent of gross domestic product, as well as the large investment in high technology at the expense of personnel, particularly in the army.

On the economic side, Australia came through the Asian financial crisis with increased strength and confidence. Its economy performs regularly at or near the top of the Organization for Economic Cooperation and Development group in terms of growth and is expected to continue to grow at a healthy 3.5–4 percent in 2000.

Australia strongly identifies its security with the stability of the surrounding region, particularly to its north. In recent decades, Australia has sought to develop and maintain working relationships with its neighbors, paying special attention to Indonesia.

The onset of the Asian financial crisis disrupted these relationships to varying degrees. Indonesia was hardest hit economically, and the economic crisis brought political difficulties as well. Australians saw the fall of Suharto in 1998 as an opening for democratization that could eventually allow relations to run more smoothly. In the short term, however, uncertainties multiplied.

The region's financial crisis coincided, within the Indonesian state, with surging separatist pressures in East Timor, Aceh province, and Irian Jaya, and with communal strife elsewhere, notably in eastern Indonesia. Concerns were raised about the possibility of Indonesia fragmenting. There was also fear that rising nationalist sentiments might create the environment for a new seizure of power by the Indonesian military.

Indonesia's problems made clear to Australia how much the stability of Indonesia is in Australia's own interest. Separatism and civil strife in so close a neighbor could affect Australia in many ways—an influx of refugees, insecurity of sea lanes, demands for intervention—in both the short and long term.

When it became apparent that new Indonesian President B. J. Habibie was prepared to grant independence to East Timor, Australian opinion was divided. Those who saw democratization in Indonesia as positive for Australia tended to consider East Timor a "sideshow." Others argued that this was a "once-in-a-generation" opportunity to resolve the East Timor issue, which had long troubled Australia's relationship with Indonesia.

East Timor itself poses no threat to Australia's security, nor does Australia have territorial ambitions there. In fact, Australia recognized the incorporation of East Timor into Indonesia de jure a decade ago. The Australian government decided, however, that if East Timor chose independence, that wish should be respected. Australia makes a sharp distinction in this regard between East Timor, as a former Portuguese colony rather than a part of the Dutch East Indies, and other Indonesian provinces where there are separatist movements.

Australia has closely followed the evolution of democracy in Indonesia. The election of President Abdurrahman Wahid and Vice-President Megawati Sukarnoputri was welcomed, along with the cabinet they appointed. Even so, new waves of violence or a displacement of the elected government by military rule could be expected to again raise tensions between the two countries.

A major consequence of the East Timor turmoil has been strain in Australia's bilateral relations with Indonesia. As the leader of the diplomatic campaign for action and as the largest contributor to the international force, Australia became the natural focus for Indonesian nationalist sentiments. The damage to bilateral relations, including Indonesia's cancellation of the 1995 treaty of security cooperation, will take many years to repair and will be dependent on processes of political change within Indonesia over which no foreign country has significant influence.

Australia's growing preoccupation with Indonesia and East Timor during 1999 led to greater attention to Australia's immediate region and thus to some reordering of its security concerns. The Association of Southeast Asian Nations (ASEAN), which Australia has long regarded as a positive factor in the region's security, and other regional institutions were able to do little when violence erupted in East Timor. ASEAN is now seen as having lost momentum generally, due to the economic difficulties of its members, weaker leaders, unresolved issues concerning decision making, and an impasse on issues where differences among members are large. It is not clear how ASEAN can return to its former vigor.

The shift in relations among major powers within the Asia Pacific region continues. This is a matter of some anxiety to Australians. It is necessary—and can be stabilizing—for Japan and China to develop regional roles, but Japan's choice of role remains uncertain, and China's pressure on Taiwan and its assertive claims in the South China Sea area could lead to confrontation. In this context, the U.S. commitment to the security of the region is regarded as vital, particularly given the tension over Taiwan and continued concern over nuclear and missile development by North Korea. The U.S. role in the region has strong support in Australia.

Australia's security is also increasingly affected by nonmilitary factors.

People smuggling and undocumented refugee movements have emerged as a significant problem, with criminal organizations drawing clients from as far away as Afghanistan, East Africa, and Iraq. Such pressures heighten Australia's sense of insecurity and reinforce the perceived need for military capability.

DEFENSE POLICIES AND ISSUES

DEFENSE POLICY   As a result of the East Timor turmoil, Australian defense policy is now formally being reviewed. The government has undertaken to produce a new policy document.

The current official policy, which dates from 1997, places greater emphasis on Northeast Asia and directly addresses the possibility of contributing to allied efforts in South Korea and the Taiwan Strait. The policy assumes a continuing stability in Southeast Asia, which would afford Australia such a shift in disposition. Domestic support might then be gained for high-technology acquisitions to enhance the country's "knowledge edge"—that is, the application of information technology to intelligence, command systems, and surveillance—and facilitate interoperability with allied forces.

Overall defense spending has been held to 1.8 percent of GDP in 1999–2000 and expected to fall to 1.7 percent in 2000–2001. Resources have been directed strongly toward investment for the future, rather than current consumption. Top priority has been given to moving to "the forefront of the revolution in military affairs." This approach is intended to exploit Australia's developed economy and high skill levels, thereby compensating for limitations on manpower numbers.

Second priority goes to developing capabilities for dealing with threats to Australia's maritime approaches—superiority in the air and augmentation of surface and subsurface maritime capability.

Third priority is developing the capability to "operate proactively" against enemy forces through such means as the F-111 aircraft and accompanying standoff weapons.

Of fourth—and noticeably lower—priority is the development of ground capability to counter threats to Australian territory. The focus here has been to develop highly mobile task forces, a limited amphibious capability, improved land surveillance capability, aerial fire support and reconnaissance helicopters, additional light-armored vehicles, and—for special forces—improved means for counterterrorism.

The government, relying on the Reform Program to shift resources from support or lower-priority matters to combat-related areas, had planned to reduce the Australian Defense Force (ADF) to a regular strength of only 42,500 troops. Under pressure from the ADF, the government modified this objective and has adopted 50,000 troops as the target. Further, a decision in April 1999 to raise a second brigade to a high level of readiness involved increased costs on the order of A$500 million (US$325 million at A$1 = US$0.65). These two changes have necessitated a far-reaching restructuring of the Reform Program.

The East Timor crisis demonstrated the limitations of the ADF resources available to deal with even a nearby problem. Australia undertook to provide up to 4,500 troops to the multinational force. As this represented a maximum effort for Australia's ground forces, concern about the size of the contingent has been expressed.

In response to the East Timor crisis, late in 1999 the government introduced a special tax levy to raise A$1 billion (US$650 million) for the army to add two battalions and for the air force to add some 350 personnel. The proposal received immediate bipartisan support.

THE DEFENSE BUDGET   The defense budget for 1999–2000 was essentially unchanged in real terms from 1998–1999, with total outlays of A$11,093 million (US$7,210 million), or 1.8 percent of GDP. (However, the 1999–2000 budget was framed for the first time on the basis of full accrual costs, including a capital use charge of 12 percent per year, which makes comparisons with previous years less clear.)

It was originally intended that the increased readiness of a second brigade-sized army group and supporting naval and air units would be financed through savings generated by the Reform Program. These savings could not be achieved by the target date at the end of June. Strains in the defense organization were evident, and several top-level officers and officials left the organization. When the 1999–2000 budget was presented, the subject of personnel numbers for the regular Defense Force was "under detailed review."

A total of A$3,578.6 million (US$2,326 million), or 32.26 percent of defense outlays, is devoted to investment. This comprises A$73.6 million (US$47.8 million) to be spent on new projects and A$3,505 million (US$2,278 million) for ongoing projects.

Major new capital equipment projects, representing a total cost of A$2,285.2 million (US$1,485 million), are as follows:

• Reconnaissance and fire-support helicopters

- Intelligence support
- Joint command support
- Military geographic information system
- Air-to-air missiles
- Minesweeping and mine-identification enhancements
- F-111 electronic countermeasures
- Ground force vehicle life extension
- Air combat training system
- Seasparrow missile upgrade
- Air-to-surface weapons.

Projects already approved include:

- Anzac frigates
- Lead-in fighters
- Helicopters for the Anzac frigates
- Strategic airlift
- P3 maritime surveillance update
- New Collins-class submarines
- Coastal mine-hunters
- Communications upgrade
- Seasparrow missiles
- Jindalee over-the-horizon radar
- Surveillance night-fighting equipment
- F/A 18 Hornet fighter upgrade
- Missile decoys for ship protection
- Tactical air defense and control radars.

The government recognizes that there is a short-term as well as a continuing need to boost defense resources. The higher levels of readiness are expected to be maintained at least until 2001. There is also the prospect of obsolescence of major equipment, such as F/A 18 and F-111 aircraft and naval destroyers and frigates. These major capital needs could require up to A$35 billion (US$23 billion) over the next ten to fifteen years.

Nonmilitary security needs also demand increased funds. With 37,000 kilometers of coastline and nine million square kilometers of ocean to cover, the government was obliged to react to growing illegal immigration and quarantine breaches. Following a review, an additional A$124 million (US$81 million) over a period of four years has been allocated to coastal surveillance and related services. Actions to be taken include increased air patrols, improved coordination with the customs service, expanded liaison with countries from which illegal immigrants originate and through which they travel, legislation to strengthen maritime investigatory and enforcement powers, and support for a protocol on people smuggling to be added to the proposed UN Convention on Transnational Organized Crime.

ALLIANCE RELATIONSHIPS   The ANZUS alliance with the United States and New Zealand continues to have high profile in Australia, with the East Timor situation the dominant focus in 1999. There were close consultations on issues and responses. When pressure grew for a multilateral force, the Australian government made clear that it was looking for "boots on the ground," but the United States indicated it was willing to provide only limited, noncombat support. U.S. support did increase from its initial offer, but it did not include combat elements and was less than Australia had wanted.

These developments led to a public airing of differences. While visiting Australia, the U.S. secretary of defense stated that the United States had received no formal request for combat forces, prompting a clarification from the Australian government that it had been clear from informal exchanges that any such request would be declined. However, Australia subsequently stated that the ADF accepted the U.S. contribution to the East Timor operation as fully satisfactory. Regardless of whether communication was less than perfect, or expectations on the part of the Australian government were unrealistic, it seems that Australia needs to adjust its notions of alliance support in the event of security problems within its own neighborhood.

The formal expression of U.S.-Australian solidarity came in the form of the ANZUS communiqué, issued on November 3 after the annual Australia–United States Ministerial Consultations, held in Washington and attended by both the U.S. secretary of state and secretary of defense. On most international security issues in the Asia Pacific, there was close alignment between the two countries.

Australia's security relationship with New Zealand is predominantly bilateral and proceeds under the Closer Defense Relations program, which seeks to enhance cooperation and interoperability between the forces of the two countries. Again, the dominant concern during 1999 was East Timor. New Zealand was one of the first to offer combat forces, which it subsequently increased to a full battalion when Australia raised its own commitment to 4,500.

CONTRIBUTIONS TO REGIONAL AND GLOBAL SECURITY

East Timor remains the major regional security issue for Australia. Earlier Australian interest in assisting East Timor has been strengthened by Australia's close involvement with the process that led to East Timor's opting for independence. Proposals made by Australian Prime Minister John Howard to Indonesian President Habibie in December 1998 regarding the future of East Timor played a part in Habibie's January 1999 offer of autonomy to East Timor. At a subsequent meeting in Bali, Howard and Habibie discussed the referendum, including the key question of security in the face of increasing violence in East Timor.

When violence exploded in East Timor after the UN poll, which showed 78 percent of the population in favor of independence, public opinion in Australia demanded that the government seek multinational intervention for peace enforcement, beyond conventional peacekeeping. Australia also played a key role in the discussions of East Timor at the annual Asia-Pacific Economic Cooperation (APEC) meetings, in Auckland, and at the associated ad hoc meeting of foreign ministers on East Timor. The 7,500 troops-strong International Force in East Timor (INTERFET) that was ultimately assembled was led by an Australian commander and included a large Australian contingent.

Support for the multinational force was nearly universal within the Australian community, but bipartisan support for the policy that led to intervention has been elusive. Criticism has centered on the accuracy of government assessments of the likelihood of violence and the lack of early and effective Australian lobbying of the United States and others to have a peacekeeping force in place before the referendum.

When Indonesia formally agreed to independence for East Timor in October 1999, the UN Transitional Administration in East Timor (UNTAET) was established. Australia has sought to reduce its role in this phase of peacekeeping, while shifting its emphasis to humanitarian assistance and reconstruction. In the 1999–2000 fiscal year, Australia has committed A$75 million (US$48.88 million) to reconstruction and development assistance to East Timor—a level of support that is expected to continue for the remainder of East Timor's transition to independence. It is likely that Australia will need to contribute substantially to East Timor's development for the foreseeable future.

Elsewhere within the region, Papua New Guinea (PNG), where there has been long-term deterioration, continues to be a source of serious concern for Australia. In early 1999, desperate to retain power, the PNG prime minister approached Taiwan, asking for assistance in return for a change in Papua New Guinea's China policy—a change that Australia feared could have unsettling consequences for the region. Elections in July brought to office Sir Mekere Morauta, possibly the best qualified and most highly regarded PNG prime minister in many years, but the Morauta government faces serious challenges to its reformist policies. Australia pledged credits of A$120 million (US$78 million) to help the new government stabilize Papua New Guinea's financial position.

On the troubled island of Bougainville, where Papua New Guinea has been resisting a separatist movement for the last decade, Australia is the leader of the 300-strong regional Peace Monitoring Group. An arrangement involving a high degree of autonomy for Bougainville is under consideration, and Australia is looking to reduce its involvement gradually.

Australia continues to be involved in regional multilateral dialogues in such groups as the ASEAN Regional Forum, and it participates in the Korean Peninsula Energy Development Organization and in the Five Power Defense Arrangements with Malaysia, New Zealand, Singapore, and the United Kingdom.

2 Brunei Darussalam

THE POLITY Brunei Darussalam is the smallest state in Southeast Asia, with a population of about 330,000. The labor force is about 120,000, half of whom are immigrants. Brunei nationals are the overwhelming majority in the public sector (more than 90 percent of the total), while foreigners dominate the private sector (about 75 percent). The country's only major developed natural resources are large offshore oil and gas deposits, which have made possible a high per capita income of about US$15,000.

Brunei attained full independence from Britain in 1984. Its late entry into the world of sovereign states is partly explained by its size and concern for security without British protection. Brunei chose to maintain a low international profile and appeared to adopt a reactive foreign policy. Participation in the Association of Southeast Asian Nations (ASEAN) facilitated necessary political-economic interactions and acquisition of experience in international affairs. Recent events have generated greater interest and involvement in external affairs. New regional institutions like the Asia-Pacific Economic Cooperation (APEC) forum and the ASEAN Regional Forum (ARF) have provided platforms for Brunei's emergence as a more active member of the international community.

Brunei is a highly traditional society, with a hereditary monarchy and a state religion, Islam, which is practiced strictly. At the same time, Brunei can also be considered a modernizing society.

SECURITY Since independence, Brunei's leaders have not had to deal with domestic threats or political instability. The 1990s have seen a continuation of the environment of the 1980s, with a generally satisfied population benefiting from generous government programs and enjoying one of the highest standards of living in the Muslim world. Minor instances of discontent reported in the local media are basically individualistic in nature; no collective political action has been organized to date. A few avenues for political participation are available. There is one registered political party, the Brunei National Solidarity Party (PPKB), which works within the prescribed rules of the political system. Three daily newspapers have opinion pages that provide a channel for political expression and do affect the public agenda. Foreign publications circulate freely as long as they do not impinge on local sensitivities regarding religion and the monarchy. Satellite radio and television transmission is available.

The most significant event influencing Brunei's political security environment was its experiment with democracy in the early 1960s while still a British protectorate. Elections for Legislative Council were held in March 1962, but after a rebellion in December that year, the council was suspended. The rebellion was led by the Brunei People's Party (PRB), the most successful political party in the election, which opposed Brunei's entry into the Malaysian federation and demanded changes to the domestic political system. British Gurkha forces flown in from Singapore quickly crushed the insurrection. Although thirty-eight years have passed since this incident, and it is rarely discussed in public, its impact continues to be felt in the political arena.

The wave of democratic reform in some ASEAN countries has not posed any serious challenge to the sultanate and its concept of a "Malay, Islamic monarchy." Brunei's 1959 constitution, suspended after the rebellion in 1962, is still on hold; the country is governed under emergency rule renewed every two years. However, a constitutional review committee was established in 1996. The committee reportedly has submitted its recommendations, including the reinstatement of some features of the 1959 constitution and some form of popular elections. The fact that the hereditary monarchy is willing to consider new institutions and processes after sixteen years of independence indicates movement toward opening up the political system, even if basic features of the hereditary system are likely to be retained.

While oil and gas have been the mainstays of the economy, accounting for almost all export earnings and slightly more than half the national income, revenue from past capital investment has also contributed a growing share of the national budget in recent years. Regional and global economic developments have affected Brunei, although not to the same extent as its neighbors. Its currency, on par with the Singapore dollar, has depreciated about 15 percent against the U.S. dollar since the end of 1997. More significant was the drastic drop in global oil prices, which reached US$9 per barrel in 1998 before recovering to US$23 in mid-1999 and US$25 by the end of the year. Government expenditure was tightened and some infrastructure projects were shelved in 1998, and the gross domestic product growth rate was about 1 percent during that period. The very large Amedeo Development Corporation collapsed, leaving huge debts estimated at over US$10 billion to both domestic and foreign creditors. The recovery of oil prices in 1999 was a blessing for this single-product export economy.

THE REGION   Brunei is bifurcated by the Malaysian state of Sarawak, but no political insecurity appears to have arisen from this fact. Brunei's historical claims to the territory of Limbang and its differences over the demarcation of parts of the common border have been pursued through diplomatic channels.

Brunei enjoys close ties with Malaysia and Indonesia. Developments in 1998–1999 in both these countries—the dismissal of Deputy Prime Minister Anwar Ibrahim and ensuing tensions in Malaysia, and the instability brought on by political change in Indonesia—caused concern in Brunei. While not commenting officially on these matters, which it considered the internal affairs of these countries, the Brunei government offered financial assistance to both neighbors through bilateral as well as multilateral aid and investment. The economic turmoil in Indonesia led to a small number of immigrants and job seekers entering Brunei illegally, but the flow subsequently eased. A more significant impact of the Asian economic crisis on Brunei was the departure of foreign workers as private and public projects were curtailed, leading to a slump in the retail and property sectors.

The Brunei government also regarded the East Timor issue as a strictly internal Indonesian matter. Brunei did not comment on the crisis, or on the International Force in East Timor (INTERFET). However, part of the British military contribution to INTERFET came from the Second Gurkha Battalion, which has remained in Brunei since the early 1980s under a bilateral treaty with the United Kingdom. Brunei's media gave prominent coverage to the departure of the "brave Gurkhas" for East Timor in September 1999 and to their return in December.

Increasing activities under ASEAN and the ARF have expanded the

worldview of Brunei policymakers and military leaders. The legal rami-
fications of the country's Exclusive Economic Zone under the UN Convention on the Law of the Sea, the conflicting territorial claims in the
South China Sea, and the continuing problems related to the Spratly Islands have influenced the security analyses of the political and defense
establishments.

DEFENSE POLICIES AND ISSUES

DEFENSE DOCTRINE   According to a statement by the Ministry of Defense, which was established in 1984, "The main thrust of the national
defense policy is to preserve the independence, security, national sovereignty, peace, territorial integrity, and the national interest of Brunei
Darussalam." Aside from this general policy statement, the Brunei government has not issued a defense doctrine or white paper on security
and defense policy. However, the comments of various policymakers
suggest the general thrust of Brunei's defense policy: that Brunei is a
small state that poses no threat to anyone and, as it has no harmful intentions, it expects the same in return.

Brunei officials repeatedly emphasize that diplomacy is the country's
first line of defense—quiet diplomacy and nonaggressive styles of behavior. Government leaders often state that ASEAN is the cornerstone of
Brunei's foreign policy.

This premium on friendly external relations has not, however, created an air of complacency in policy-making circles. Brunei's defense
thinking has clearly undergone changes over the past decade. In the first
ten years of independence, there was confidence that nonintrusive external policies coupled with special ties with the United Kingdom would
handle major security needs. Since the mid-1990s, more concern has been
evident. A landmark was Brunei's 1994 agreement with the United Kingdom, the Memorandum of Understanding on Defense Procurement,
which provided for hardware purchases for the air force and navy and
for the modernization and expansion of existing facilities. This was an in-
dication of Brunei's taking on more responsibility for guarding its vital
resources and its exposed coastline and for meeting any provocations.

NEW DEFENSE PERCEPTION   The departure of Britain from Hong
Kong in 1997 did not directly affect the bilateral defense link between
Britain and Brunei. The British Gurkha Garrison, a legacy of the 1962

Gurkha airlift from Singapore, remains in place at the oil town of Seria, eighty kilometers south of the capital Bandar Seri Begawan. A Brunei-U.K. agreement for stationing the Gurkha Battalion was signed in 1983 and has been renewed every five years. There was some uncertainty about the future of the garrison as the 1997 handover of Hong Kong to China approached, because the battalion in Brunei rotated with the battalion in Hong Kong every six months. The impending withdrawal, combined with the reduction in Britain's Gurkha battalions—from seven to two as of 1994, one of which was moved to the United Kingdom after the Hong Kong handover—led to Brunei's decision to retain the garrison in Brunei.

BRUNEI ARMED FORCES   The last three years have seen major changes in Brunei's armed forces. From the mid-1960s, the air force and navy were integral parts of the Royal Brunei Armed Forces. In 1991, the defense organization was restructured, but the air force and navy received their official colors only in April 1996.

EQUIPMENT   Brunei's armed forces are modestly equipped, although modernization is planned over the next two to three years. The Land Forces consist of infantry battalions with light armored tanks and surface-to-air missiles. The navy has coastal missile craft and inshore and river patrol boats. The air force has no combat aircraft as yet, but it does have three helicopter squadrons, a flight school with various training capabilities, and a transport squad. The major function of the air defense battery is to protect the capital, the international airport/air

Table 1. Brunei Security Forces

Structure	Royal Brunei Land Forces	
	Royal Brunei Air Force	
	Royal Brunei Navy	
	Royal Brunei Services Force	
	Royal Brunei Armed Forces Training Centre	
Strength	Total	about 5,000
	Land Forces	3 battalions, about 4,000 troops*
	Air Force	3 helicopter squadrons, 400 troops*
	Navy	700 troops
Reserves	Land Forces	700 troops
Internal security	Police	1,750 officers

* Estimates only; battalion or squadron size may not be the same as the standard British battalion or squadron.

Table 2. Foreign Security Forces in Brunei

British Garrison	Gurkha Unit	1 battalion, about 800 troops
	British personnel in command and training and technical services	200
Gurkha Reserve Unit		2 battalions, 2,300 troops
Singapore Armed Forces	Jungle training, at Temburong camp	500–800 troops
	Helicopter detachment, at Bandar air base	
	Administrative/support staff, at Bandar	500

force center, and the naval base at Muara. Air and naval defense capability will be upgraded over the next two years with the arrival of fighter jet aircraft, Sikorsky Black Hawk and Bell helicopters, and better equipped naval vessels. Personnel are now undergoing training.

BUDGET   The police force comes under the Prime Minister's Office, while the armed forces and the Gurkha Reserve Unit are under the Ministry of Defense.

In the last few years, the Ministry of Defense has had the highest level of ordinary expenditure of any ministry. From 1995 to 1997, defense spending increased from B$405 million (US$676.4 million at US$1 = B$1.67) to B$548 million (US$915.2 million). By comparison, the Ministry of Education's budget was only B$347 million (US$579.5 million) in 1997, and Brunei's total ordinary expenditure for 1997 was about B$2.6 billion (US$4.3 billion).

Brunei's Seventh National Development Plan (1996–2000) allocates B$528 million (US$881.8 million) to developmental expenditures in the security sector, 7.3 percent of the total. It is estimated that of this total, B$466 million (US$778.2 million) is for the armed forces; twenty-eight projects, representing about two-thirds of the total, were reported to be either completed or in their final stages by 1999. This allocation covers buildings and other facilities only; the amounts spent for weapons and equipment are not made public.

The Brunei government maintains the British Garrison (the Gurkha Battalion) in Seria at an estimated (unverified) cost of about US$25 million per year for personnel and equipment. The garrison is entirely under British command; thus, for example, the recent deployment of the forces to East Timor was purely a British decision.

As a result of falling oil prices and the default of Amedeo, the local construction company, Brunei's development budget was reduced by about 20 percent in 1998. This cut evidently affected the planned purchase of jet aircraft for the air force and expansion of the air base adjacent to the international airport, as well as the acquisition of new naval craft.

PARTNERS IN DEFENSE   Brunei maintains close military ties with a number of countries for defense procurement, technical services, training of personnel both within and without Brunei, and general military advice. In addition to the United Kingdom, partner countries include Australia, Canada, France, Germany, Indonesia, Malaysia, New Zealand, Singapore, and the United States. Several bilateral memoranda of understanding have been signed in the past decade in various areas of military cooperation.

Of Brunei's partners, the United Kingdom is of special significance, not only as a source of arms procurement but also for its role in providing training and technical expertise. British personnel work in Brunei on loan from the British military, while civilian personnel from Britain and elsewhere work under contract with the Brunei government. British officers also command the Gurkha Battalion.

Singapore has had close military relations with Brunei since the early 1970s, when it established a camp in Temburong for jungle warfare training. At any one time, there may be about 500–800 men in training, in addition to officers and staff who maintain a permanent site in Bandar for logistics and coordination with the local military. A helicopter detachment is mainly for purposes of transport.

The U.S. military, especially the Pacific Command, makes regular visits to Brunei. Brunei has expressed support for a U.S. military presence in the Asian region and has agreed to provide access to visiting naval forces.

Brunei does not yet have any military link with China, although it has pursued close diplomatic and economic ties with China since establishing formal relations in September 1991.

CONTRIBUTIONS TO REGIONAL SECURITY

Brunei defense officials believe that Brunei should contribute in whatever way it can to the stability and security of the Southeast Asian region.

This would be done primarily through maintaining a viable military force, small but modern and capable of defending any territorial incursions. Brunei believes that each ASEAN member should likewise contribute its appropriate share to ensuring security.

Brunei, however, does not see itself as a leading player in regional issues. Its size does not permit significant participation in international undertakings, but it has shown support where possible. It sent twelve police personnel as observers to the UN-supervised Cambodian elections of 1993, and a half dozen civilian and military observers for the 1998 elections. Brunei did not offer direct assistance to the UN-sponsored INTERFET mission in East Timor in 1999, and has not indicated if it will participate in the UN Transitional Administration in East Timor (UNTAET). However, it will likely contribute humanitarian relief, probably through the UN High Commissioner for Refugees (UNHCR), as it did to the Kosovo Relief Fund.

Brunei's support for a constructive U.S. role in the region and its hosting of a British military presence helps these two powers in case of a need to project force. The British contribution to INTERFET of Gurkha soldiers from the British Garrison is an example of this.

While maintaining close bilateral ties with Australia, Malaysia, New Zealand, Singapore, and the United Kingdom—signatories of the 1971 Five Power Defense Arrangements (FPDA)—Brunei has not indicated an interest in joining this multilateral security group. Nevertheless, it has been invited as an observer to FPDA military exercises. The only other multilateral security-oriented group in which Brunei participates is the ARF, which since 1995 has offered an opportunity for the Brunei government to interact with some twenty other governments on regional security issues. As Brunei does not yet have academic or research institutions, its participation in the multilateral security dialogue is limited to government representatives from the foreign and defense ministries.

By participating in regular bilateral military exercises with the armed forces of its neighboring countries, Brunei has also built up good relationships both at top leadership and military levels. Despite its very limited military power, Brunei hopes through this network of quiet defense diplomacy to help achieve security within and without Southeast Asia.

3 Cambodia

The Security Environment

Cambodia enters the year 2000 with a new sense of optimism. The previous year was significant in terms of defense and foreign policy as this once war-torn country moved away from its preoccupation with domestic affairs. Cambodia has opted for a foreign policy of constructively engaging the region and the world beyond; it has also shifted to a more multilateral approach. In defense policy, Cambodia is downsizing its armed forces and working to define new strategic priorities based on the concept of comprehensive security.

At the broader level, however, Cambodia will take a long time to normalize its participation in the regional and global community. Important domestic issues remain, including building a basic national consensus and defining the appropriate role of the military.

INTERNAL   For the first time in recent history, Cambodia is enjoying relative peace, political stability, and security. Greater internal stability has allowed more attention to be devoted to national reconstruction and economic development.

After two decades of civil war and outside intervention that claimed two to three million lives, the Paris Peace Accord of October 1991 made possible a UN-organized election in 1993. The election was closely contested, with the royalist party FUNCINPEC winning the most votes and the Cambodian People's Party (CPP), drawn mostly from the former communist People's Republic of Kampuchea (PRK) government, coming in second. This outcome led eventually to a coalition Royal Government of Cambodia, with former ruler Prince Norodom Sihanouk as king and head of state, FUNCINPEC leader Prince Norodom Ranariddh as first prime minister, and CPP leader Hun Sen as second prime minister.

The coalition collapsed in an outbreak of fighting in July 1997, only to be reestablished in November 1998, due in part to international pressure. In the new arrangement, the CPP became the dominant partner in the coalition. Prince Ranariddh was made president of the National Assembly, Hun Sen was named prime minister, and a new Senate was established to complement the National Assembly in reviewing legislation.

Although Cambodia still faces daunting political challenges in developing a viable national consensus, the new coalition worked successfully in its first year. Several factors seem encouraging for the future political development of the country. First, there is increased acceptance of the role of a legitimate opposition, which is a new feature of Cambodian political life. The opposition Sam Rainsy Party challenges the government vigorously on almost every issue in the National Assembly.

Second, Cambodia is moving forward with holding local elections for the first time in its history. The government has prepared a draft local election law for National Assembly consideration. Through popular elections at the grass-roots level in 2000, there is now the prospect of a more decentralized political system in the country.

Finally, compromise and the resulting stability in the political arena paved the way for renewed international financial support. The Consultative Group meeting in early 1999 brought US$470 million in pledged assistance. By the end of 1999, the International Monetary Fund and the Cambodian government began renegotiating a loan agreement that had been suspended in 1996. Stability, combined with good weather, also led to a rice surplus in 1999–2000, improving food security.

Among the near-term challenges, Cambodia is still seeking to integrate former Khmer Rouge soldiers into the Royal Cambodian Armed Forces (RCAF). Another sensitive challenge involves trials for Khmer Rouge leaders accused of human rights atrocities. Finally, with King Sihanouk's worsening health, increasing focus is being given to the royal succession. Constitutionally, the Throne Council chooses a new king, but the politics of succession are untried and complex. Although the CPP appears likely to have some influence over the selection, the four major candidates are all royalists. These include the queen; prince Ranariddh; Prince Sihamoni, the ambassador to UNESCO in Paris; and Prince Sirivudh, the king's half brother. Some Cambodians, however, question the need for the monarchy.

EXTERNAL   The substantial support received by Cambodia from the international community has changed Cambodia's strategic outlook. Most Cambodians accept that the country cannot remain isolated and underdeveloped, and must become a part of the region and broader Asia Pacific community. Cambodia's membership in regional institutions and its strengthened international relationships make for a more benign external environment. Nevertheless, Cambodia's international relations still contain numerous problematic elements.

Cambodia and the United Nations. An initial UN effort to negotiate peace in Cambodia in 1979 failed due to cold war politics. The Vietnam-installed and Soviet-backed PRK was in power in Phnom Penh. The opposition Coalition Government of Democratic Kampuchea (CGDK), a loose alliance of the Khmer Rouge, Prince Sihanouk's ANKI (Independent Khmer National Army) group, and Son Sann's Khmer People's National Liberation Front, was supported by China, the United States, and the Association of Southeast Asian Nations (ASEAN). The CGDK occupied Cambodia's UN seat until the Paris Peace Accord in October 1991. This alienated leaders of the PRK who held important positions in the current government. Moreover, the results of the UN-organized 1993 election were a disappointment for former PRK members of the CPP, which finished in second place.

After the 1993 election, the United Nations maintained two offices in Cambodia: the Office of the Special Representative of the Secretary General and the UN High Comissioner for Human Rights (UNHCHR) in Cambodia. In September 1999, Prime Minister Hun Sen asked that the Office of the Special Representative be closed when its mandate expires in early 2000, on the grounds that the Cambodia Mission to the United Nations could handle these functions. He agreed to extend the UNHCHR office until 2001.

A complication in Cambodia's relations with the United Nations is the proposed trial of the former senior leaders of the Khmer Rouge. In 1997, the coalition government requested UN assistance in arranging a trial. After delays due to the 1997–1998 political crisis, in 1999 the United Nations recommended an international tribunal. King Sihanouk supported this approach, but the Hun Sen government expressed preference for a trial in Cambodia under Cambodian law. The government has drafted its own law for the trial, which could start as early as March 2000. Apparently it will rely on experts from France, Russia, and other countries, but it will not follow the UN proposal.

ASEAN. In 1999, Cambodia finally became a full member of ASEAN, culminating a long process and symbolizing Cambodia's full acceptance by its neighbors.

Cambodia had become an official ASEAN observer in 1995. It was scheduled to become a full member along with Laos and Myanmar in July 1997, but this was postponed because of the outbreak of fighting in Cambodia. An ASEAN troika, consisting of the foreign ministers of Indonesia, the Philippines, and Thailand, continued to engage Cambodia until the new coalition government was formed as a result of the 1998 election. The 6th ASEAN Summit, held in Hanoi in December 1998, approved Cambodia's admission, which was formalized later in April 1999. Cambodia's membership completes the ASEAN-10. Cambodia also intends to join the Asia-Europe Meeting at the organization's third meeting to be held in Seoul in 2000.

Relations with China. With a long history, including King Sihanouk's close personal relations with former Chinese leaders, the relationship with China is critical for Cambodia. After the 1997 fighting, Second Prime Minister Hun Sen closed the Taiwan Trade Representative Office in Phnom Penh. A deal with Eva Airways to open routes between Taipei and Phnom Penh was scrapped as well. Subsequently that year, China extended military assistance to Cambodia, in the form of military trucks and jeeps, as well as humanitarian aid.

In 1998 and 1999, China's investment flows and tourist arrivals to Cambodia increased substantially. High-level visits also increased. Prime Minister Hun Sen and members of his cabinet, the co-defense ministers, and the commander-in-chief of the RCAF all are recent visitors to China. In October 1999, the Chinese embassy in Phnom Penh provided the venue for an informal meeting between Hun Sen and Prince Ranariddh. Other events included Cambodia's condemnation of the U.S. bombing of the Chinese embassy in Belgrade and the reaffirmation of its "one China" policy after Taiwan President Lee Teng-hui's comment on "state-to-state relations."

Sino-Cambodian relations experienced some tension in late 1999 when Cambodia grew concerned over increasing numbers of illegal Chinese immigrants using Cambodia as a transit point to third countries. The governor of Phnom Penh arrested hundreds of Chinese immigrants, which upset China. After approaches by the Chinese embassy in Phnom Penh, the immigrants were allowed to return to China.

Relations with the United States. Other than the period between 1993 and 1997, Cambodia's relations with the United States in recent decades have generally not been good. Cambodia remembers the U.S.

bombing of the country during the Vietnam War and the U.S. support for the Khmer Rouge in the 1980s. Strain resumed with the July 1997 fighting, which led the United States to terminate defense cooperation and reduce aid. From approximately US$40 million annually, U.S. aid has fallen to US$10 million, mostly for humanitarian purposes.

December 1999 saw two positive developments in Cambodia-U.S. relations. The United States donated one hundred army trucks to the Cambodian Mine Action Center and two other mine clearance organizations, and in response to a Cambodian request, the United States imposed a ban on trade in Cambodian antiquities. However, the forthcoming trial of the Khmer Rouge leaders could again complicate relations; the United States favors a UN trial, while the Cambodian government wants a Cambodia-based trial.

Relations with Thailand. Cambodia's relations with Thailand are complicated by historical issues as well as unresolved problems such as land and maritime borders, trade, and immigration. Cambodia's perception that Thailand supported the Khmer Rouge was a thorn in the relationship before the Khmer Rouge collapsed in late 1998. Since then, relations have improved, with an increase in official visits and cooperation in tourism, trade, customs, defense, and rail transportation. In October 1999, King Sihanouk presented Cambodia's highest awards to two Thai generals for their assistance throughout the 1980s and the recent strengthening of military ties along the border. In December, Prime Minister Hun Sen and other cabinet members visited Thailand.

The outstanding issue now is the border. In 1998, Cambodia protested a bilateral maritime agreement between Thailand and Vietnam that affected Cambodia's maritime border and its Exclusive Economic Zone in the Gulf of Thailand. During 1999, Cambodian media reported that Thailand had encroached on Cambodian territory, particularly in areas formerly under the control of FUNCINPEC and the Khmer Rouge. This led to student demonstrations and a call by King Sihanouk for a special meeting. Other issues included border trade, especially smuggling, and the landing of an artillery shell in Cambodian territory during the Thai-U.S. Cobra Gold exercises.

Relations with Vietnam. Cambodia-Vietnam relations have a difficult history and many challenging issues, including land and maritime borders, immigration, and border trade. Some of these issues will take time to resolve and require serious negotiations.

Nevertheless, Cambodia-Vietnam relations improved in 1999, principally through high-level visits. In December, Vietnamese Deputy

Defense Minister Le Vandung led a military delegation to Cambodia, meeting with Prime Minister Hun Sen, Co-Defense Minister Tea Banh, and RCAF Commander-in-Chief Ke Kim Yan. The visit focused on the border issue and military cooperation between Hanoi and Phnom Penh. Cambodian and Vietnamese leaders want to conclude an agreement on border demarcation by the end of 2000.

DEFENSE POLICIES AND ISSUES

In the post–Khmer Rouge period, Cambodia has no significant internal enemies or serious external threats. The official view is that Cambodia must think strategically and pursue a "defensive defense strategy." In 1999, the Ministry of Defense began working on a defense white paper, drawing on the existing Five Year Plan for 1999–2003. This will lay down the military framework and outlook for Cambodia.

OBJECTIVES   Key current defense objectives are to restructure Cambodia's armed forces and to define the military's strategic priorities, missions, and role in peacetime.

Although the precise size of Cambodia's armed forces is difficult to determine, the Five Year Plan calls for a reduction in military personnel from 140,000 to 85,000, in addition to a reduction of police forces from 65,000 to 41,000. The reduction is to be implemented gradually. Divisions in the armed forces are to decrease from twenty-six to fewer than ten, with consolidation to take place in several areas. Relocation, however, will be a challenge due to the lack of facilities as well as communication and transportation problems.

The military's new role, based on the concept of comprehensive security, will emphasize border protection, acting as an intervention force to help police and custom officials fight smuggling, and providing emergency support, disaster relief, and humanitarian assistance.

BUDGET   Cambodia's defense budget is spent primarily on salaries and basic needs such as food, uniforms, and fuel, rather than on arms and equipment.

The defense budget is not published, but reportedly the combined 1999 "defense and security" budget, which includes military and police, was about US$122 million, roughly 41 percent of the national budget. This represented a slight real increase from US$119 million in 1998, which was 48 percent of the total budget. For 2000, the budget is to drop to US$119 million, 37 percent of the total. Of the 1999 defense and security budget, about US$91.5 million is estimated to be for the military alone. In 2000, this figure is expected to decrease to US$89 million.

Cambodia has been under pressure from the donor community to reduce its defense and security expenditures in favor of areas such as health and education. However, despite the shifts, defense and security are still projected to be the largest single budget item.

DEMOBILIZATION AND REINTEGRATION   The matter of demobilization needs to be addressed more fully. Unless achieved in a timely manner, there could be serious repercussions for the country. As it is, it will be expensive, estimated to cost up to US$100 million, largely because of the reintegration of the demobilized soldiers and police into society. The donor community—especially the World Bank and the Japanese government—has raised critical questions concerning the effectiveness of demobilization to date.

FORCE STRUCTURE   Cambodia's regular armed forces numbered approximately 140,000 for the military and 65,000 for the police in 1999. Cambodia also had about 32,000 "special status" forces, which served as communal militias. Unofficial estimates of Cambodia's military forces by year and category are given in table 1.

Table 1: Personnel Strength of Cambodia's Military Forces

	1997	1998	1999
Regular Forces			
Police	67,800	65,700	65,000
Military	123,100	143,300	140,000
Special Status			
Military Militias	27,900	7,500	Demobilized
Communal Militias	31,500	32,100	32,000

DEFENSE PROCUREMENT   Cambodia's purchases of defense equipment and weapons are not substantial. Further, only a small amount is spent on repairing existing military equipment. As of 1999, Cambodia's military arsenal included two small ships, five functioning Czech-made

L-39 aircraft used only for training, one AN-24 aircraft, four MiG-21s undergoing repairs in Israel, three helicopters, one Y-12 aircraft, over twenty tanks and antipersonnel carriers, and more than three hundred army trucks.

DEFENSE COOPERATION   Since 1993, Cambodia has had defense cooperation arrangements with a number of countries. China has provided military trucks and jeeps. Before July 1997, the United States provided military training and humanitarian assistance. France supplied pickup trucks, military schools, and training for the military police. Canada assisted in mine clearance training. Australia supported Cambodian participation in the ASEAN Regional Forum (ARF), provided English-language schools and training for peacekeeping operations, and assisted in the preparation of a defense white paper. Thailand provided parachute training for the military in its border areas. Malaysia provided training for navy personnel as well as ship repairs. Indonesia trained Cambodia's Special Force 911 and Parachute Commandos. During the 1997 fighting, some of these arrangements were suspended or terminated.

CONTRIBUTIONS TO REGIONAL AND GLOBAL SECURITY

As a small country emerging from years of war and conflict, Cambodia cannot contribute significantly to regional and global security at this time. However, the fact that Cambodia is no longer a "running sore of Southeast Asia" is already a contribution to regional and global peace.

GOOD NEIGHBOR POLICY   Since 1993, Cambodia has pursued a "good neighbor" policy to help build confidence and trust. The primary objective is to enable the country to devote its time, resources, and energy to national development. But it should contribute to regional resilience as well.

THE GREATER MEKONG SUBREGION (GMS)   A key member of the GMS—other members are Laos, Myanmar, Thailand, and Yunnan province of China—Cambodia has been actively promoting peace, cooperation, and development in the subregion. Peace and cooperation could attract tourism and foreign investment into the area, while development of the GMS could lead to greater peace, security, and prosperity for all members.

ASEAN AND ARF   Cambodia hopes its membership in ASEAN and the ARF will enable it to contribute more actively to regional peace and security. Specifically, Cambodia believes its neutral position could help build confidence and trust on these issues among the states making conflicting claims in the South China Sea.

PEACEKEEPING AND LAND MINES   When Indonesia asked Cambodia to participate in the UN peacekeeping operation in East Timor, Prime Minister Hun Sen declined on the grounds that this would constitute interference in internal affairs. However, given its own experience with UN peacekeeping, Cambodia should eventually be able to contribute to other international peacekeeping operations. As a country with firsthand experience with land mines, Cambodia has already shared its knowledge of this problem—from treating victims to mine clearance—with Bosnia and Kosovo. Cambodia is a strong proponent of a comprehensive ban on land mines.

4 Canada

As they enter the twenty-first century, Canadians feel a general unease concerning their overall security. While they perceive no conventional military threat to their country, in a recent nationwide poll 60 percent of the Canadian public indicated a belief that the world is now a more dangerous place than it was during the cold war. They also expressed increasing concern over whether Canada can continue to play a distinctive, positive role on the world stage.

In 1999, the Canadian public's attention was captured by four headline events:

- Interdiction of three unregistered vessels attempting to smuggle 590 Chinese immigrants into Canada;
- Participation by Canadian forces in the North Atlantic Treaty Organization's (NATO's) Kosovo bombing campaign;
- Dispatch of Canadian peacekeeping forces to distant East Timor; and
- Apprehension at the U.S. border of individuals who had used Canada as a staging ground for terrorist bomb plots against U.S. targets.

Taken as a whole, these events brought home to Canadians the continental, regional, and global dimensions of their post–cold war security concerns.

Despite high-profile efforts by the government in the UN Security Council and elsewhere, Canadians feel a rising frustration. Humanitarian tragedies continue unabated, especially in Africa; international nuclear nonproliferation regimes appear to be eroding; transnational

47

criminal activities are gaining momentum and having an impact on Canadian society; and the results of a decade of diminishing commitment to the Canadian military have begun to be felt.

GLOBAL SECURITY CONCERNS   In broad terms, Canadians are concerned that the international security order shows signs of renewed competition among the major powers. Bilateral relations among the United States, China, and Russia are not on an even keel, and the foreign policies of all three are subject to unpredictable domestic developments. While the prospect of direct conflict among them remains very slight, since the early 1990s there has been a reluctance to cooperate in managing regional conflicts and sustaining international arms control regimes. Indeed, Canadian concern over weapons of mass destruction has increased. Traditional crisis points remain in South Asia and North Korea. China is seeking to modernize its arsenal; so is Russia, even as it has only tenuous control over its aging nuclear inventory. With the Comprehensive Test Ban Treaty (CTBT) not ratified by key countries, prospects for the Nonproliferation Treaty (NPT) renewal conference are not good.

Canadian priorities in both security and economics are to promote the establishment and effective operation of multilateral institutions and to ensure a role for middle powers in rules-based, international governance. Thus, on the economic front, while clearing the way for Chinese entry into the World Trade Organization was seen as an important step, the impasse at the November 30–December 3 meeting in Seattle demonstrates the daunting challenges for international economic reform in the next decade. At the regional level, the North American Free Trade Agreement has brought mixed results for Canada—there has been significant integration into the North American (that is, the U.S.) economy but also an increase in trade disputes with Washington. As for the Asia-Pacific Economic Cooperation (APEC) forum, while Canada remains committed to the goals of freer trade, it is concerned that there has been little progress over the last several years.

REGIONAL SECURITY CONCERNS   Canada's regional security concerns are widely dispersed, but common themes are managing intrastate conflict and advancing regional security institutions. In the Americas, Canada has supported democratization and human development through its membership in the Organization of American States and its participation in peacekeeping and peace building in the Caribbean. Canada remains dismayed at the human destruction and failures of governance in Africa, and it has attempted through the British Commonwealth and (to a lesser extent, with the Francophones) to bring pressure to bear on outlaw governments. In 1999, Canada was active in promoting efforts to reenergize regional and UN initiatives for peace in Africa.

Canada's most extensive institutional ties are in Europe, built around its NATO membership. The Canadian government was a firm supporter of NATO action in Kosovo, a campaign that the foreign minister defended as advancing human security and that the Canadian forces touted as demonstrating their interoperability with sophisticated U.S. and European forces. While overt conflict has been quelled in the Balkans, continued outside assistance and peacekeeping missions will be necessary for many years. Ottawa wants to be assured a voice in regional counsels commensurate with its contribution to regional security, which it feels was denied at key moments in the Yugoslavian crises of the 1990s. The unpredictable nature of the Russian government, conflicts along the Russian periphery, and the potential for resurgent militarism persist. Engaging Russia as a partner in regional affairs remains difficult, due in part to Russia's suspicion of NATO enlargement and resentment of unilateral action taken by NATO and the United States.

Canadian interests in Asia Pacific derive from economic, political, social, and security linkages to the region. While the Canadian economy as a whole is on the upswing, industries involved with Asia are depressed. The large Asian communities living in Canada continue to grow, and have a tendency to replicate within themselves the divisions that exist in their homelands. This has sometimes led to violence, posing a domestic security concern for Canadian authorities. Attention to trans-Pacific criminal networks in drug trafficking, money laundering, the sex trade, and people smuggling also continues to increase.

Canadian concerns regarding Asia Pacific stability focus on the lack of an effective, inclusive regional security architecture. Progress in this regard, on economic and security dimensions, on regional and subregional levels, and in track one (ASEAN Regional Forum [ARF]) and track two (Council for Security Cooperation in Asia Pacific [CSCAP]) modes, seems to have stalled in recent years. In part, this is an understandable consequence of the Asian economic crisis. However, in Northeast Asia and in South Asia, the Korean peninsula, Taiwan, and Kashmir security problems appear to be entrenched. While North Korea is seeking to open relations with new states, including Canada, and has halted its missile testing programs, there are no signs that the North Korean government is prepared to undertake meaningful reform or to engage the Kim Dae Jung administration in South Korea.

Geopolitics dominates the policies of the major powers, although a form of concert-like summit diplomacy has emerged among them. In Southeast Asia, the differences among member states of the Association of Southeast Asian Nations (ASEAN) appear more pronounced, posing considerable problems for effective cooperation. The stability and integrity of Indonesia are a primary concern; Canadian analysts regard the domestic political situation as highly volatile. Resolution of the East Timor crisis has been difficult, and the viability of an East Timorese state is in serious doubt.

CONTINENTAL SECURITY   Partnership with the United States on defense and security matters has been a cornerstone of Canadian policy, cemented in the NATO alliance and numerous North American defense agreements. This relationship will remain fundamental to the Canadian national interest. However, tensions arose between Ottawa and Washington during 1999. A series of incidents highlighted immediate transnational security threats. These included thefts of U.S. weapons technology, the breach of computer networks, illegal trafficking of money, drugs, and people, and at year-end the discovery of anti-U.S. terrorist activities in Canada. Elements in the U.S. Congress have expressed concern that Canada may be a "weak link" for the United States because of Canada's extensive, largely unpatrolled sea and land borders, and because of perceived Canadian laxness or inability to move against transnational crime. One result was the U.S. withdrawal of long-standing exemptions of Canadian firms from licensing requirements for defense products. Despite extensive negotiations, this issue was unresolved at the end of 1999, putting at risk billions of dollars of Canadian defense contracts. U.S. authorities have also threatened to impose rigorous cross-border security checks, which could paralyze transborder economic traffic.

Broader policy issues have also emerged with the United States. These largely reflect divergent national attitudes on global security matters. For example, the United States has responded to the potential threat from rogue states by pursuing development of theater missile defense (TMD) and national missile defense (NMD) systems, but Canadians question whether Canada should participate in these NMD efforts. Canadians are also concerned about the extent to which NMD and TMD development threatens the global nonproliferation regimes, specifically the Anti-Ballistic Missile (ABM) Treaty, as well as stability in Asia Pacific. U.S. refusal to ratify the CTBT, U.S. reluctance to participate in UN peacekeeping missions, and perceived U.S. tendencies toward unilateralism have only underscored these questions. Conversely, the current Canadian government's emphasis on the human security agenda has been a dilemma, even an irritant, for Washington.

THE NEW SECURITY AGENDA   The most notable shift in Canadian foreign and defense policy over the last decade has been the adoption of a human security perspective on international affairs. For the author of this view, Foreign Minister Lloyd Axworthy, human security places priority on the well-being and rights of the individual: "Conceptions of global peace and security based primarily on national security are no longer sufficient." Promotion of human rights, intervention on humanitarian grounds, and emphasis on democracy, development, and peace building have become central priorities for Canadian policy. The government has challenged its NATO allies to revise the organization's nuclear weapons doctrine, pushed for the establishment of an international criminal court, and broadened its campaigns from antipersonnel mines to protest small arms proliferation, child soldiers, and similar issues. These priorities do not always sit well with Canada's allies, whether regional or major powers. Largely undeterred, and frustrated over the international community's inability to avert tragedies during the 1990s, Axworthy and Prime Minister Jean Chretien have sought to develop "middle power initiatives" and "coalitions of the willing" to respond to human security crises. Canada's human security commitment, however, does not rule out the use of military force to intervene in another state, even without UN sanction, if compelling humanitarian reasons are seen to exist. This was the case with Kosovo.

DEFENSE POLICIES AND ISSUES

Canada remains officially committed to its 1994 defense white paper and to the maintenance of "multi-purpose, combat-capable forces" deployable around the world. However, since 1994 the uniformed armed forces have been cut by 30 percent to 60,000, and civilian support by 45 percent. Nevertheless, the Canadian forces maintain a high operational profile. In 1999, more than 4,000 troops were deployed abroad in peacekeeping missions, including some 1,400 in Bosnia and initial deployments of 600 in East Timor and 1,000 in Kosovo. This proved to be unsustainable, and the prime minister finally admitted that the "costs involved and lack of capability to respond" required a rationalization in Canadian commitments abroad. The Kosovo unit is being reduced to a token 100 personnel; the longer-term total for Canadian peacekeepers abroad is now set at 3,000.

The reductions have essentially been budget driven. Defense purchasing power has fallen by more than 30 percent in the 1990s. The allocation of 6.1 percent of government spending to defense is a historic low. At about 1.1 percent of gross national product, this is sufficiently below the 2.1 percent NATO average to provoke public criticism from NATO head Lord George Robertson. However, 1999 may have marked a turning point. For the first time in the decade, the defense budget rose—by Can$400 million (US$276 million at Can$1 = US$0.69) to a total of Can$9.7 billion (US$6.69 billion). Of this total, Can$175 million (US$120.75 million) was earmarked to address "quality of life issues" of Canadian service personnel.

As for capital equipment, Canada is taking delivery of four Victoria-class diesel-electric submarines from the United Kingdom. It has recently received or contracted for search-and-rescue helicopters, light armored personnel carriers, and reconnaissance vehicles—the latter two to provide better support for peacekeepers. Some Can$1.4 billion (US$966 million) has been committed to upgrading the air force's CF18 fighters. However, major purchases remain delayed, particularly a much-needed maritime helicopter to compliment the frigates built in the 1990s.

Procurement decisions due early in this decade will have a crucial effect on the Canadian forces. These involve (a) naval supply and airlift capacities, (b) new fighter aircraft, (c) adaptation to the technological "revolution in military affairs" (RMA), and (d) engagement in American continental missile defense plans. Ottawa has been slow to address the RMA issue; its first major study was produced in 1999. Another recently issued study projects Canadian security and defense issues to the year 2020. Despite growing public debate on the NMD issue, the government's position is that this is under review and no decision has been made.

In addition to the peacekeeping missions noted above, Canadian forces have sustained their activities with their European security partners. In 1999, Canada hosted a NATO exercise involving more than 15,000 personnel. In the Pacific, the navy's annual ship visit program (WESTPLOY '99) took place in Southeast Asia, and exercises were conducted with Australian and U.S. partners. Canada hosted a Japanese naval visit in 1999. Canada's contribution to the multinational East Timor force included transport planes, troops, and a naval supply vessel.

CONTRIBUTIONS TO REGIONAL AND GLOBAL SECURITY

GLOBAL SECURITY   Canada assumed its seat on the UN Security Council in January 1999, announcing its intention to invigorate council proceedings by giving priority to human security issues, promoting transparency and openness in what was seen as a major power club, and prodding the council to take seriously its responsibility to respond to crises in a timely and effective manner. Canada's record to date has been mixed. While chairing the council, Canada sponsored sessions on human security issues. Robert Fowler, Canada's UN ambassador, has been an outspoken critic of UN failures to reform and respond, while at the same time taking the lead in seeking an effective role for the UN in the Angola crisis. (However, Canada subsequently found itself in the awkward position of having acquiesced in the NATO-driven decision not to seek Security Council sanction for its Kosovo campaign.)

Concerns have risen in Canada in recent years regarding international nonproliferation regimes. With the South Asian nuclear tests, U.S. refusal to ratify the CTBT, and the stated intention of some U.S. politicians to circumvent or violate aspects of the ABM Treaty in order to deploy missile defense systems, there appears to be a reversal of momentum. Canada is actively preparing for the upcoming NPT review. It has attempted to initiate dialogue with the South Asian countries, though with little success. As with its human security agenda, Canada's strategy on nonproliferation has been to form coalitions of like-minded states to bolster existing regimes or to establish new ones. During 1999, Canada succeeded in attaining sufficient ratifications (89) among the 136 signatories to bring into effect the Ottawa Convention banning antipersonnel mines. This achievement, however, has been tempered by the refusal of the United States and other major powers to sign the convention and by continuing use of mines in intrastate conflicts such as Angola and Kosovo.

Canada's human security agenda includes both existing programs and new initiatives. Control of small arms is now receiving priority attention, along with efforts to protect the welfare of civilians in war environments and to ban the recruitment of child soldiers. Peace building is also being emphasized; the government has allocated Can$125 million (US$86.25 million) for projects working toward this end. Many of these projects involve working with nongovernmental organizations, rather than official institutions, both in Canada and abroad.

REGIONAL SECURITY   Canadian support for the peacekeeping mission in East Timor has been noted. In general terms, Canada has continued its efforts to be seen as a relevant, engaged player in Asia Pacific, particularly in multilateral security dialogue mechanisms at both the official and unofficial levels. Canada has worked hard to energize various components of the ARF, CSCAP, and other dialogues. Foreign Minister Axworthy has called for "ASEAN's collective voice . . . to be heard in global forums" on issues, such as drug trafficking, that have specific relevance for Southeast Asia. Canada's Can$100 million (US$69 million) in assistance to the region supports a wide variety of activities, including the annual Asia Pacific Round Table, training and institution building seminars, and projects on building civil society. Canada participates in CSCAP activities, especially the North Pacific Working Group, which it cochairs with CSCAP Japan. CSCAP remains the only "full house" security dialogue in Northeast Asia, regularly engaging North Korea as well as Mongolia.

Canadian officials admit that Asia has proven to be somewhat "stony ground" for the human security agenda. Asian governments, academics, and experts remain suspicious of the concept, concerned that it has interventionist overtones, represents Western values, and advances the interests of Northern, developed countries. Efforts to justify the recent Kosovo campaign as a human security initiative have not helped in this regard, especially with China. Even so, Asian governments have been receptive to certain aspects of the human security agenda, such as post-conflict peace building. In some countries, such as Thailand and the Philippines, Canadian civil society efforts are regarded quite positively. However, Canadians are increasingly concerned about the state of civil society in Malaysia, where Canada has had substantial involvement in the past.

Canada also pursues key bilateral relationships, particularly in Northeast Asia. Over the last five years, considerable effort has been invested in Canada-Japan cooperation on security matters. Regular political-military talks are now held, high-level visits have increased, and a seminar of experts, officials, and academics is now held every two years. Canada has established a program of annual track two workshops with

China, engaging participants from the foreign ministries, academies, and universities in discussions of the theory and practice of security multilateralism.

Finally, Canada has given special attention to engaging North Korea in subregional security dialogue. Since 1990, Canadian academics have periodically visited North Korea and hosted North Korean delegations to Canada. These efforts promote North Korean participation in multilateral dialogue and have laid the groundwork for regular official contacts. At the same time, Canada also continues to support the Korean Peninsula Energy Development Organization (KEDO) effort to restrain North Korean nuclear development.

5 China

As China enters the year 2000, its leaders have grown worried about its security environment. At home, 1999 saw economic difficulties and slowdown, the political campaign against Falun Gong, and the "two states" remark by Taiwan's Lee Teng-hui. Globally, due to the war in Kosovo and the bombing of the Chinese embassy in Belgrade, China's leaders perceive a negative turn of events. While convinced that peace and development remain the major global trends, China is nevertheless seriously concerned about American unilateralism, power politics, military action by the North Atlantic Treaty Organization (NATO), the weakened role of the United Nations, and "humanitarian intervention" into the internal affairs of states.

INTERNAL   The celebration in October 1999 of the fiftieth anniversary of the People's Republic of China (PRC) was a positive event in an otherwise difficult year. The economy has slowed, the political landscape is harsh, and there is trouble in cross-Strait relations.

After maintaining 7.6 percent economic growth in 1998 despite the Asian financial crisis, China's growth rate slowed to 7.1 percent in 1999. This was high by global and regional standards, but lower than China's average over the last twenty years. There are economic difficulties in four major areas. The domestic market is weak, with low personal spending and deflation. Foreign investment has declined by 9 percent. Exports grew only 2.1 percent in the first nine months of 1999. And there has been no fundamental change in the condition of state enterprises. State enterprises still account for 44 percent of economic output and absorb large governmental subsidies and bank loans, but are unprofitable and inefficient.

The government made determined efforts to stimulate the economy. It increased spending on public projects, raised the pay of eighty million civil servants by roughly 30 percent, and increased benefits to the retired and unemployed. To encourage domestic spending and investment, it lowered interest rates. At the annual Communist Party Central Committee meeting in September, targets and principles for state enterprise reform and development through the year 2010 were set. The National People's Congress passed a constitutional amendment upgrading the status of private enterprise in order to stimulate growth in the private sector. It also imposed a tax on interest from bank deposits, both to encourage people to spend money and to increase state revenues. The practical outcome of these measures remains to be seen.

Domestically, China engaged in a major political campaign in 1999. Seeing a threat from the growing Falun Gong spiritual movement, the Chinese leadership banned the organization. Falun Gong had become the largest organized group in China after the Chinese Communist Party and may even have surpassed the party in numbers. In the seven years since Falun Gong was founded in 1992, membership had grown to two million (the government figure) or one hundred million (according to the organization). Falun Gong staged demonstrations, sit-ins, and boycotts in several Chinese cities, the largest demonstration occurring in Beijing on April 25, at Chinese Communist Party and government headquarters, involving ten thousand to twenty thousand participants. Upon banning of the organization in July, the government launched an intensive propaganda campaign denouncing Falun Gong; it arrested the group's leaders and put them on trial.

Another political issue was the statement by Taiwan leader Lee in a July 9 interview that relations between Taiwan and mainland China should be on a "state-to-state" basis. Viewing Lee's statement as a step toward declaring Taiwan's independence, PRC President Jiang Zemin demanded that Lee retract his statement. Beijing postponed a planned trip to Taiwan by Wang Daohan, president of the Association for Relations Across the Taiwan Strait (ARATS), the organization managing Beijing's relations with Taiwan. Jiang set two conditions for rescheduling the visit: that Lee retract his "two states" formula, or that Wang meet Lee in the capacity of chairman of the Nationalist Party (KMT), not as president of Taiwan. Beijing, however, expects no progress on this issue until after Taiwan's elections in March 2000.

In early September, the Chinese military held landing exercises in coastal Zhejiang Province and southern Guangdong Province. Attended by the vice-chairman of the Central Military Commission, the exercises were intended to demonstrate that the Chinese military had improved its joint combat capacity and was prepared to crack down on any separatist acts.

Macao returned to PRC sovereignty on December 20, 1999. With Hong Kong having returned in 1997, this leaves only Taiwan as the only separated part of China. There has been increased discussion about the "timetable" for Taiwan's return. President Jiang, Vice-Premier Qian Qichen, and other Chinese leaders have stated that Taiwan's reunification with the mainland cannot be delayed too long. However, no Chinese official has specified a date for Taiwan's return. Showing goodwill toward the people of Taiwan when an earthquake devastated Taiwan on September 21, President Jiang and ARATS immediately extended their condolences. Along with the Red Cross Society of China, the government offered various forms of assistance to Taiwan, including US$100,000 in relief funds and 500,000 yuan (US$60,000 at 1 yuan = US$0.12) worth of relief materials.

EXTERNAL   Compared with the uneasy domestic economic and political situation, China's external environment is generally good. However, the bombing of the Chinese embassy in Belgrade on May 8, 1999, which killed three and wounded more than twenty, generated a major crisis between China and the United States. Many Chinese believe the attack was intentional. Most Chinese believe American weapons too advanced to hit the wrong target, and they discount excuses about "old maps." A perceived lack of sincerity in apologies by U.S. President Bill Clinton, U.K. Prime Minister Tony Blair, and NATO officers immediately after the incident only strengthened Chinese suspicion. The Chinese government did not formally conclude that the action was intentional, but it did not accept the American explanation and continues to seek more information.

Following the attack, large demonstrations occurred in Beijing, Shanghai, Guangzhou, Shenyang, Chengdu, and elsewhere, causing damage to American embassy and consulate buildings. The mass reaction was an expression of years of Chinese frustration and anger over American actions such as sanctions after Tiananmen in 1989, the sale of one hundred fifty F-16 aircraft to Taiwan in 1992, Lee Teng-hui's visit to the United States in 1995, the sending of two aircraft carriers to Taiwan in 1996, and charges of Chinese political donations and theft of American nuclear technology. The Chinese government declared that it had not organized the demonstrations, but rather had managed and controlled the expression of these pent-up feelings. At the official level, contacts with the American government were restricted for more than four months, American naval ships were not permitted into Hong Kong harbor, and military-to-military relations were cut off.

The Kosovo war and embassy bombing prompted serious, wide-ranging debate on China's foreign policy in speeches by leaders, newspaper editorials and articles, and journals. Did Deng Xiaoping's assessment of the global strategic situation still apply? Were peace and development still the major global trends? What is the China strategy of the United States and the West? Is multipolarity the global trend? What is the role of the United Nations? What should China's international role and foreign policy be? After a couple months of debate, however, the Chinese leadership affirmed Deng's view of the global situation and the fundamental points of China's foreign policy. China's leaders still believe that China as a developing country should concentrate on development and maintain good relations with all countries, including the United States and other Western nations.

China and the United States resumed high-level contacts when Jiang and Clinton met at the Asia-Pacific Economic Cooperation (APEC) meeting in Auckland in mid-September. A compensation agreement was reached at the end of the year, in which the United States would pay US$28 million for damage to the Chinese embassy and China would pay US$2.7 million for damage to U.S. buildings in China. The agreement was helpful, but relations between the two countries have not fully recovered. The process of resuming military-to-military contact is slow, and dialogue on human rights issues has not formally begun again.

A serious casualty of the embassy bombing was Sino-American negotiations on China's entry into the World Trade Organization (WTO). The two sides had made significant progress during Premier Zhu Rongji's visit to the United States in early April, Zhu indicating that the agreement was 95 to 99 percent complete. Clinton, however, worried about congressional resistance, would not conclude the agreement. Another round of negotiations was held immediately after Zhu's visit, but the embassy bombing in May disrupted the talks. Jiang and Clinton resumed the WTO discussions in Auckland in September, but there was no breakthrough. The process remained deadlocked until Clinton called Jiang on November 7. Three days later, U.S. Trade Representative Charlene Barshefsky and National Economic Council Director Gene B. Sperling led an American delegation to Beijing, and after six days of intensive negotiations, an agreement was reached.

China's relations with Russia, Japan, the two Koreas, the member countries of the Association of Southeast Asian Nations (ASEAN), and others were, on the whole, positive in 1999. Relations with Russia became closer because the two countries shared similar positions on Kosovo. Political and military ties were strengthened by regular high-level political and military exchanges. A joint statement issued during Russian President Boris Yeltsin's visit to China in December supported multipolarity and the Anti-Ballistic Missile (ABM) Treaty, and condemned the development of national missile defense systems. Russia supported the return of Macao and Chinese reunification, and China supported Russia over Chechnya. Agreements on border demarcation were signed, including provision for joint economic use of some islets and their surrounding waters in border rivers.

China's relations with Japan and India did not change in 1999, but tensions on particular issues such as history and nuclear testing were reduced. China continued to oppose the Guidelines for U.S.-Japan Defense Cooperation, urging Japan to adhere to its Peace Constitution and maintain a defense-only policy.

China signed long-term cooperation documents with Thailand and Malaysia. China and the Philippines had disputes over construction and fishing issues in the South China Sea, but the two countries agreed to control their differences. Following discussions during Zhu's visit to Vietnam in December, China and Vietnam signed a treaty on their land border.

China congratulated ASEAN for admitting Cambodia into the organization and realizing a ten-nation association. China supports ASEAN as an important regional force that promotes economic development, regional dialogue and cooperation, and peace and stability. Zhu attended ASEAN's summit meeting in November in Manila.

In the post–cold war era, China's foreign and security policies have become much more Taiwan-centered; that is, China judges other countries heavily on their position regarding Taiwan. The government and military regard the Taiwan independence movement, and foreign support of this movement, as a major threat to China's security and sovereignty. This is the fundamental reason for China's current position on

U.S. forward deployment in the West Pacific, the U.S.-Japan security alliance, and the development of theater missile defense by the United States and Japan.

Lee Teng-hui's remarks concerning "two states" did not cause major diplomatic tensions between China and other countries because almost all countries support a "one China" policy. Clinton's timely call to Jiang following Lee's statement proved reassuring and good damage control. The Chinese government was sufficiently satisfied with the response of the international community not to take military or diplomatic action against Taiwan.

In mid-December, however, China and the United States again quarreled over Taiwan. China protested Clinton's support of Taiwan's "participation" in the World Health Organization. Chinese Foreign Ministry officials accused the United States of violating the three Sino-U.S. joint communiqués and the U.S. commitment not to support Taiwan's efforts to join international organizations of sovereign states.

DEFENSE POLICIES AND ISSUES

THE NEW SECURITY CONCEPT   China continues to seek a "new security concept." At the ASEAN Regional Forum (ARF) annual meeting in July in Singapore, Foreign Minister Tang Jiaxuan spoke on the basic points of China's new security concept. Chinese scholars continued to develop the concept, publishing articles on new theories of international security such as comprehensive security, cooperative security, human security, economic security, common security, and mutual security.

DEFENSE SPENDING   According to the state budget passed by the National People's Congress in March, China's defense spending in 1999 was 104.55 billion yuan (US$12.55 billion), an increase of 12.7 percent over the previous year. This was not a dramatic increase, given the government's promise to increase the official budget allocation to compensate for the security forces' disengagement from commercial business as of 1999.

ORGANIZATIONAL CHANGE   The three-year reduction of 500,000 personnel from the People's Liberation Army (PLA) is scheduled for completion in 2000. It has been reported that 81,000 officers left the military in 1999. Military education was reorganized; non-command academies and schools such as engineering, medical, and logistics were combined into a smaller number of institutions. A further change was the decision to replace the PLA's decades-old service-oriented logistics system with a "joint logistics service" system in 2000.

The annual Communist Party Central Committee meeting in September added three members to the Central Military Commission (CMC), the highest military decision-making body in China. One was Hu Jintao, PRC vice-president and a Politburo Standing Committee member, who was named a vice-president of the CMC; after Jiang, he is only the second civilian to serve on the commission.

MILITARY MODERNIZATION   In August, the Xinhua News Agency announced that China had conducted successful tests of a new long-range ground-to-ground missile. China successfully tested its first manned spacecraft in November. An official spokesman stressed that China's space technology is purely for peaceful, not military uses.

China does not publish information on its military modernization or weapons acquisition programs. However, reports in *Jiefangjun Bao* (Liberation Army Daily) indicated that the Chinese military was engaged in military modernization programs, and Jiang and other leaders repeatedly urge the armed forces to use science and technology for modernization. The National Day parade on October 1 displayed new army, navy, air force, and strategic force weapons, including new intercontinental ballistic missiles and fighters.

SOUTH CHINA SEA   No major developments occurred in 1999 in the South China Sea. However, China and the Philippines engaged in a dispute over "new construction" on the Meijijiao (Mischief) Reef in the Nansha (Spratly) Islands early in the year. The Philippines government criticized the Chinese action as violating a 1998 agreement. China denied any new military construction and offered joint use of the facilities built on the reef. The Chinese government believes that the Philippines highlighted the issue mainly to pressure the Philippines Senate into passing a new Philippines-U.S. Visiting Forces Agreement.

During his visit to the Philippines in November, Premier Zhu reiterated China's support for peaceful settlement of these issues through negotiations based on international law. A Chinese spokesman denied rumors that China had turned down an ASEAN draft code of conduct for the South China Sea, stating that, on the contrary, China had recently given ASEAN its draft and that China was willing to work with

ASEAN on such a document. However, China stressed that this agreement should only apply to the Nansha Islands area, where most disputes occur, as the inclusion of other areas would complicate matters. China and the ASEAN countries will continue their discussions on the code of conduct in 2000.

MISSILE DEFENSE   China continued to criticize development of theater missile defense (TMD) and national missile defense systems by the United States and Japan, which China sees as designed to "strengthen both their sword and shield to gain their own absolute security." Government and military leaders raised this issue with American counterparts throughout the year. In November, the English-language *China Daily* reported the statement of Sha Zukang, director of the Department of Arms Control and Disarmament of the Foreign Ministry, that "China does not reject the whole concept of theater missile defense." China understands the value of TMD to protect stationed troops, but it opposes systems that can be used in national missile defense. Sha asserted the lack of necessity for Japan to join the American TMD, and stated that China will not tolerate an attempt to bring Taiwan into TMD.

China and Russia held talks on missile defense, issuing a joint statement of their "serious concerns" over the American plan to deploy antimissile systems. China also joined with Russia in efforts at the United Nations to press the United States to abide by the ABM Treaty.

China has two major concerns on missile defense. First, it suspects that the United States will provide missile defense to Taiwan, enhancing Taiwan's capability against the Chinese mainland and encouraging or protecting Taiwan's independence. Missile defense could also link the American and Taiwanese militaries more closely. Second, missile defense will force China (and other countries) to spend more on both offense and defense, causing increased military spending and a kind of arms race China does not wish to see.

ARMS CONTROL   China has not changed its long-standing position on nonproliferation, arms control, and disarmament, continuing to fulfill its obligations under multilateral and bilateral agreements. However, its tone on these issues changed with the Kosovo war and the crisis in Sino-U.S. relations caused by the embassy bombing. The Chinese delegation to the first Conference on Facilitating the Entry into Force of the Comprehensive Test Ban Treaty (CTBT) in October indicated that

China will try to speed up ratification of the treaty and regrets the lack of participation by some parties in the treaty organization's preparatory work. The Chinese government urged the United States to ratify the CTBT.

CONTRIBUTIONS TO REGIONAL AND GLOBAL SECURITY

KOREA   The Chinese government welcomes the positive changes in the situation on the Korean peninsula and the progress in North Korea–U.S. relations through the Berlin agreement on missiles and bilateral relations. China believes the Four-Party Talks (between it, North and South Korea, and the United States) are "useful and productive."

China and both Koreas improved their relations in 1999. In the summer, China hosted a delegation led by Kim Yong-nam, president of the Presidium of the Supreme People's Assembly of North Korea. This was the first high-level delegation to China since the death of Kim Il-sung. Chinese leaders expressed support for North Korea in its efforts to normalize relations with the United States, Japan, and the European Union, and for the independent and peaceful reunification of North and South Korea. China donated 150,000 tons of grain and 400,000 tons of coking coal to North Korea during the year.

A breakthrough occurred in the relationship between China and South Korea in August 1999: the first visit by a South Korean defense minister to China. The two sides agreed to develop military exchanges.

CENTRAL ASIA   China, Russia, Kazakhstan, the Kyrgyz Republic, and Tajikistan continue the "Shanghai process" started in 1996 to promote confidence-building measures in their border areas. In August 1999, at a summit meeting held in Bishkek, capital of Kyrgyz, the five countries agreed to expand cooperation in security as well as economics, and to join in their efforts against international terrorism and national separatism. China and Kyrgyz signed an additional, separate agreement, settling all disputes over the border between the two countries.

SOUTH ASIA   China expressed regret and concern over missile tests by India and Pakistan in April, which it fears could spark an arms race in South Asia. China kept a balanced position during the fighting between India and Pakistan in the summer. Chinese leaders urged both sides to cease fighting and exercise restraint. China believes that the

Kashmir dispute can only be settled through peaceful negotiations, and urged India and Pakistan to respect the Line of Control.

ASEAN REGIONAL FORUM   The Chinese government supports the ARF, which it regards as a major institution for discussing security issues in the region. However, China does not support proposals that the ARF should move beyond the current confidence-building stage to "preventive diplomacy." China believes that the ARF should remain a security dialogue forum, not a security organization. China also insists on the noninterference principle and does not believe that the ARF or any other regional forum should have the right to intervene in the internal affairs of states unless a state accepts such intervention.

EAST TIMOR   China acted quite differently on the issues of Kosovo and East Timor. While opposing the North Atlantic Treaty Organization's (NATO's) interference in Yugoslavia's internal affairs, the Chinese government respected the choice made by the East Timorese in the referendum on independence. This was based on two factors: the East Timor referendum was arranged between Indonesia and the United Nations; and the majority of people in East Timor voted for independence and the Indonesian government accepted the result. China demanded that all violence in East Timor be stopped immediately and the security of UN personnel be protected. China cooperated in passing the UN Security Council resolution authorizing a UN peacekeeping force led by Australia. China also agreed to contribute police personnel to the operation, a rare step by China in international peacekeeping.

THE UNITED NATIONS   As the sole Asian permanent member of the UN Security Council, China attaches great importance to its role in enhancing international security. However, it has major differences with some other members of the Security Council over the principles of national sovereignty, noninterference in internal affairs, and the use of force. Thus, in 1999 China took different positions at the United Nations from the United States and other countries over Iraq and Kosovo.

China believes that Iraq has fulfilled its responsibilities under UN resolutions, sees no serious evidence that Iraq is still developing weapons of mass destruction, and favors lifting sanctions. Russia and France share this view, but the United States and the United Kingdom do not. This produced a deadlock on issues concerning Iraq and continuing U.S. and U.K. military action against Iraq, which China condemns.

On Kosovo, the Chinese government had major differences with NATO. China does not believe there was clear evidence of mass killings or ethnic cleansing in Kosovo prior to the NATO military action, and it considered the Kosovo situation an internal Yugoslav affair. China opposed NATO's military action against Yugoslavia because it lacked UN approval and conflicted with the UN Charter's principles of national sovereignty and nonintervention. Further, China believes the Kosovo precedent could give the United States and other Western countries an excuse to use force against other countries, including China, in the future. Thus, the Chinese government regarded NATO's action in Kosovo as an example of hegemony and power politics, and Chinese official news media harshly condemned NATO. China, however, did not block the UN resolution on Kosovo in July because even Yugoslavia accepted the measure.

6 European Union

European security concerns continue to be dominated by the Balkan situation. In Bosnia in 1999, tensions between the three major ethnic groups—Bosnians, Serbs, and Croats—were, somewhat tenuously, held in check by the Stabilization Force (SFOR), a large international military presence organized by the North Atlantic Treaty Organization (NATO). During spring, however, the conflict over Kosovo escalated into a massive air campaign by NATO. This campaign failed to receive a mandate by the UN Security Council, although the Security Council declared the Kosovo crisis a threat to peace and international security and did not call for a halt to the air campaign. The campaign ended with Serbia agreeing to a political settlement for Kosovo along the lines of a formula it had previously rejected. The implication of the settlement was that Kosovo, like Bosnia, would become a de facto UN protectorate. As in Bosnia, NATO organized an international security force, the Kosovo Force (KFOR), to secure the settlement.

The Kosovo campaign was interpreted by some observers in Asia as a sign that NATO was being transformed into an instrument for global military intervention. But from a European perspective, the Kosovo intervention was exceptional: Kosovo was increasingly a threat to European stability; NATO's credibility was at stake; the UN Security Council could not respond adequately because of Russian objection. America's European allies resisted U.S. efforts to give the alliance free rein without a UN mandate. NATO's New Strategic Concept, which was adopted at NATO's 50th Anniversary Summit in Washington in April 1999, reflects this European reluctance to accept the Kosovo intervention as a new paradigm.

In fact, Europe was ill-prepared militarily for the kind of contingency represented by the Kosovo intervention, let alone for global power projection. U.S. combat aircraft flew roughly 85 percent of the sorties in Kosovo, while European armies found themselves stretched to the limit by their contributions to KFOR. The crisis therefore spurred renewed efforts by the European Union to develop a common security identity and joint military capabilities.

Asia Pacific has long been a secondary security concern for Europe. In 1999, Asia Pacific security was pushed even further into the background by the events in the Balkans. Yet, as China's veto threat in the Security Council and the bombing of its embassy in Belgrade showed, the crisis in Kosovo was not confined to Europe. Nor could Europeans afford to ignore security developments in East Asia. Concerns about global order and the transregional spillover effects of interdependence emphasize Europe's important and tangible security interests in East Asia. For example, exports of technology for weapons of mass destruction or long-range missiles could easily affect European security; indeed, the export of such weapons by North Korea to the Middle East and North Africa would suggest this is already the case.

Events during 1999 further underscored the significance of security developments in East Asia. Most noteworthy was the East Timor referendum for independence and its violent aftermath. Several European countries joined in the UN operation to restore security and rebuild East Timor as an independent state. On other East Asian fronts, European security concerns continue to focus on the Korean peninsula, the European Union continues to participate in the ASEAN Regional Forum (ARF), and several EU member states are developing bilateral security relations with Japan, South Korea, and China.

Europe's involvement in the Asia Pacific region continues to be heavily defined by economics. As a result of the Asian financial turmoil, there has been a relative decline of European interest in East Asia. Trade had expanded rapidly in the years before the turmoil, and European trade with East Asia had come to approximate the total U.S. trade with the region. But with sharp contraction in several East Asian economies, 1998 exports from the European Union to East Asia fell. East Asian exports to the EU countries increased, however, suggesting that the European market, like that of the United States, played an important role in helping East Asia's economies weather the crisis. European transnational corporations, which remain less involved in East Asia than their Japanese or American counterparts, used Asia's capital needs to strengthen their presence through acquisitions. As East Asia began to recover in 1999, economic ties with Europe had not only survived but on balance emerged stronger.

European stakes in East Asia include regional stability as well as prosperity and an East Asia fully integrated in and committed to regional and global institutions. Europe would be profoundly affected, for example, if the momentum toward trade liberalization and open regionalism were lost in East Asia, or if East Asia were disengaged from active support of a strong World Trade Organization (WTO). As a trading power without substantial ability to project military power, Europe depends ultimately on a stable, well-ordered international environment with strong institutions. For this reason, the European Union has long supported Chinese membership in the WTO. However, while negotiations between the United States and China on WTO membership were successfully concluded by the end of 1999, negotiations between the European Union and China at the second EU-China summit in December 1999 failed to produce agreement.

Looking into the future, it seems clear that Europe will continue to be preoccupied with security issues close to home. Conflicts in and around the former Yugoslavia have been contained for the time being, but important issues—such as the future of current Yugoslavia (consisting of Montenegro and Serbia), domestic political evolution in Serbia, and the development of viable polities in Bosnia and Kosovo, both de facto UN protectorates—remain unresolved. The European Union's Balkan Stability Pact represents an ambitious effort to pacify the region by drawing it into the framework of European cooperation and integration. In Eastern Europe, the second Chechnya war demonstrated continuing uncertainties and risks of violence. And on Europe's southern periphery, from North Africa through the Israeli-Arab region, Turkey (a prospective member of the European Union), and eastward, there are a number of potential or actual conflicts that clearly affect European interests.

DEFENSE POLICIES AND ISSUES

DEFENSE POLICIES   The major development in European defense policies was the renewed effort to build a European security and defense identity. The core of this effort was the Franco-British St. Malo initiative of December 3–4, 1998, which was then joined by Germany and taken up within the context of the European Union. During EU summits in Cologne and Helsinki, concrete steps were taken to develop a joint military capability of about fifty thousand to sixty thousand men by the year 2003, as well as the necessary decision-making and operational machinery.

This political effort at closer military cooperation and integration was paralleled by moves toward organizing a European arms industry. The merger between the French state company Aerospatiale and the German company DASA, an affiliate of DaimlerChrysler, was noteworthy in this regard. Other developments, such as mergers or industrial alliances involving U.K. defense industries, are widely predicted.

While significant progress has thus been made toward a credible European military capability and security identity, many hurdles remain. The primary questions are the unwillingness of governments to cede their cherished autonomy in national defense; their ingenuity in devising political and practical arrangements with the United States, which is ambivalent about this enterprise; and, finally, their ability to mobilize the necessary financial resources.

For the whole of NATO Europe, defense expenditure in 1998 was lower in real terms than the previous year, and there are few signs that this trend will be reversed in the near future. Germany, in particular, is likely to see a further decline in real defense spending, forcing postponements or even cancellations in vital procurement programs. Among the major countries, only the United Kingdom has seen the decline in defense spending bottom out.

Table 1. Defense Expenditures in the European Union

Country	1997 Defense Expenditure	% of GDP	1998 Defense Expenditure	% of GDP
France	US$41,523*	3.0	US$39,807	2.8
United Kingdom	35,736	2.8	36,613	2.8
Germany	33,217	1.6	32,387	1.5
Italy	22,724	2.0	22,633	2.0
Spain	7,671	1.4	7,272	1.3
Netherlands	6,839	1.9	6,634	1.8
NATO Europe	173,383	2.2	171,359	2.1

SOURCE: *Military Balance, 1999/2000.* London: International Institute for Strategic Studies, 1999.
*U.S. dollar figures are at constant prices of 1997.

CONTRIBUTIONS TO REGIONAL AND GLOBAL SECURITY

As previously noted, European security preoccupations lie mostly within its own region. Consequently, most of its contributions to international security are also concentrated there. On balance, Europe, through its reliance on the United States for regional stability, probably remains a net importer rather than exporter of security. Although Europe in 1999 was the largest contributor to UN peacekeeping operations worldwide, those efforts were dwarfed by the peacekeeping forces deployed in the former Yugoslavia. Compared to 9,000 UN blue helmets on worldwide duty in fourteen UN peacekeeping missions as of mid-1999, SFOR and KFOR together comprised around 88,000 soldiers, most from Europe; the fourteen UN peacekeeping operations cost an estimated US$900 million in 1999, while KFOR alone cost US$10 billion. Beyond participation in UN and other peacekeeping operations, such as the multinational mission in Sinai, European contributions to global security largely involve preventive efforts, arms control, and disarmament. Contributions to crisis prevention and crisis management focus heavily on the Middle East and the former Soviet Union, where the Organization for Security and Cooperation in Europe plays an important role.

BILATERAL RELATIONS   The European Union collectively and several of its member states individually continue serious efforts to strengthen relations with Japan and China. Although economic issues dominate those relations, bilateral security dialogues are expanding, particularly with France, Germany, and the United Kingdom.

Relations with China have intensified as China's importance in the economic relationship between Europe and East Asia has grown in the wake of the Asian financial crisis. During the first half of the year, Chinese-European relations were overshadowed by the Kosovo crisis: China, together with Russia, opposed air strikes against Serbia and refused to authorize the action in the UN Security Council. A visit by the new German Chancellor Gerhard Schröder, planned before the start of the Kosovo campaign, was cut short but then supplemented with a more expansive visit in the fall. Illustrating the interdependent nature of security issues today, during his first stay in Beijing, Schröder apologized on behalf of NATO for the bombing of the Chinese embassy in Belgrade. Generally speaking, in terms of its diplomatic importance, China benefited from the repercussions of the Asian financial crisis and the Kosovo intervention and it used this opportunity to intensify its ties with Europe.

The Chinese government had proclaimed 1998 the "year of Europe," and Chinese President Jiang Zemin followed this up with an extensive visit to Europe in fall 1999, traveling to six countries. In France, Jiang and French President Jacques Chirac discussed strategic issues, jointly criticizing American plans to develop missile defenses in contravention of the Anti-Ballistic Missile Treaty and the rejection by the U.S. Senate of the Comprehensive Test Ban Treaty (CTBT). Any European government criticism of China's human rights record was muted.

Europe's relations with China thus tended to overshadow those with Japan. But the European Union held its regular summit meetings with Japan during 1999, and there also were bilateral meetings between Japanese Prime Minister Obuchi Keizō and several European heads of government. Notably, the latter included Germany, which at the end of 1999 passed on the chairmanship of the Group of Eight (G-8) to Japan. Security issues were central to several of the bilateral discussions, with emphasis on arms control and nonproliferation.

ARMS SALES   Europe continued to be an important supplier of arms to East Asian countries. During 1994–1996, the last period for which the U.S. government has produced comprehensive data, European suppliers provided roughly one-fifth of the total East Asian arms market, with Taiwan, Indonesia, South Korea, and Malaysia the principal customers. European arms sales to East Asia contracted sharply in 1998, due to the impact of the Asian financial crisis and the completion of the largest recent European-Asian arms deal, which was the sale of fighter aircraft and frigates by France to Taiwan.

DEPLOYMENTS IN ASIA PACIFIC   Of EU members, only the United Kingdom and France have direct security ties in East Asia. The United Kingdom continues to be a member of the Five Power Defense Arrangements (with Australia, Malaysia, New Zealand, and Singapore), while France retains possessions in the South Pacific (French Polynesia and New Caledonia). Only France still has a permanent military presence in Asia Pacific (4,300 men and three frigates, in addition to support ships, aircraft, and helicopters), although a small force of British Gurkha troops is stationed in, and financed by, Brunei.

OFFICIAL DEVELOPMENT ASSISTANCE (ODA)   During 1996–1997 (the last period for which comprehensive data are available from the Development Assistance Committee of the Organization for Economic

Cooperation and Development), the European Union accounted for about 42 percent of total ODA to Asia Pacific. Most of this was disbursed through bilateral programs.

MULTILATERAL SECURITY   Aside from arms sales (whose relevance to regional stability is uncertain), European contributions to East Asian security were mostly channeled through multilateral forums. In addition to its members' activities in the United Nations, the European Union continued to participate in the ASEAN Regional Forum and the Asia-Europe Meeting.

Europe was significantly involved in the East Timor situation. Through the years of Indonesian annexation, Portugal pursued diplomatic efforts to resolve the issue through the United Nations. Lisbon eventually persuaded its EU partners of the merits of its case, and in December 1998 the Council of Europe called for the withdrawal of Indonesian troops, the release of East Timorese leader Xanana Gusmão, and free elections. Europe also joined the international effort to pressure the Indonesian government to accept the results of the August 30 referendum. When the vote for East Timorese independence was met with terrorism by militias, the European Union imposed an arms embargo on Indonesia. Four European countries contributed to the Australian-led mission to pacify the area: France (500 men and one frigate), Italy (600 soldiers, transport aircraft, and one amphibious craft), Britain (600 soldiers, aircraft, and one destroyer), and Germany (200 soldiers in a medical unit with hospital facilities). The European Union, as well as individual member countries, also pledged a total of US$60 million in financial support for the UN operation to rebuild East Timor, this in addition to US$35 million already contributed for humanitarian assistance.

The European Union continued to participate in efforts to maintain stability on the Korean peninsula, including the Korean Peninsula Energy Development Organization (KEDO) project to replace North Korea's nuclear reactors. North Korea's development of weapons of mass destruction (WMD) and long-range missiles, which were discussed at length in the 1999 ARF meeting, have clear security implications for Europe. Iran, for example, allegedly is using North Korean technology to develop missiles capable of reaching Southern Europe. As part of its contribution to stability on the peninsula, the European Union has both maintained its financial support for KEDO and opened diplomatic dialogue with North Korea. At the same time, the European Union has continued its humanitarian assistance to North Korea, and has given full diplomatic support to efforts by the United States, South Korea, and Japan to draw North Korea into a constructive dialogue.

The major global security issues for the European Union in 1999 concerned the danger of proliferation of WMD and the perceived erosion of support for the United Nations. The refusal of the U.S. Senate to ratify the CTBT was widely criticized in Europe, even leading, as stated above, to China and France issuing a joint statement. Although European NATO allies joined the United States in the Kosovo intervention without an explicit mandate by the UN Security Council, this was generally understood to be an exception. Europe continued to insist on bringing the Kosovo operations back under the UN umbrella, eventually succeeding when KFOR received the endorsement of the Security Council. Europe's involvement in the UN-sponsored East Timor operation may also reflect in part the desire to compensate for the relative neglect of the United Nations in the first phase of the Kosovo crisis.

The events in Kosovo, East Timor, and the Korean peninsula underlined the new realities of globalization in the realm of security. While most security problems in the post–cold war world may be regional in their immediate implications, they also tend to produce wide ripple effects. European interests will almost inevitably be affected.

7 India

THE SECURITY ENVIRONMENT

Major challenges confront Indian security at the beginning of the new millennium. The year 1999 provided a backdrop of dramatic developments that will reverberate into the new century. It began with a domestic controversy about civilian control over the armed forces caused by the government's sudden sacking of the naval chief. In April, the national government in Delhi lost a no-confidence resolution in Parliament by a single vote. This led to a long electoral process in the largest democracy in the world. The ruling Bharatiya Janata Party (BJP, or Indian People's Party) was returned to power in October, with a bigger majority but a larger coalition. From May to July, India fought an intense but localized conflict in Kargil in Jammu and Kashmir with Pakistani "intruders." In August, the caretaker government released a draft nuclear doctrine, which spells out its vision of "minimum credible deterrence." Finally, the military coup in Pakistan in October, after eleven years of democracy, presents a new challenge to India's relations with its nuclear neighbor.

EXTERNAL ENVIRONMENT   India's immediate security environment remains highly problematic. India has a major territorial dispute with China in the Himalayas. Pakistan has disputed the accession of part of the province of Jammu and Kashmir to India, over which a low-intensity conflict has been going on since 1989. There is serious political instability, even open warfare, in other neighboring countries, including Afghanistan, Myanmar, Sri Lanka, and parts of Central Asia. This environment has created a perceived need for a more substantial military capability, including nuclear weapons and advanced delivery systems.

Relations with China. Sino-Indian relations deteriorated in 1998 after the Indian defense minister stated that China was the main potential threat to India, an assertion made to justify India's nuclear tests that year. Subsequent official statements explained that India does not regard China as an adversary, but as a great neighbor with which it would like to develop mutually beneficial and friendly relations. At the same time, India remains concerned over China's assistance to Pakistan's nuclear weapons program and the transfer of missile technology, which affect the security of South Asia. The Indian government noted, however, that during the Kargil conflict China steadfastly maintained its neutrality, emphasizing the need to resolve the problem through bilateral negotiations.

India would like to resolve its border dispute with China peacefully as well, through bilateral negotiations, as quickly as possible. India believes that agreements signed with China in 1993 and 1996 provide a reliable framework for peace and tranquillity in the border areas. Despite this, there has been no progress in finalizing the Line of Actual Control that separates the two countries in the Himalayas. At the same time, suspicion lingers as to China's real interests and policies toward India. This situation is unlikely to change until a border settlement is reached.

Relations with Pakistan. In contrast to its view of China, Indian perceptions of Pakistan hardened in 1999, after an outbreak of open conflict in May. Two rounds of structured bilateral dialogues between senior government officials in late 1998 led to a historic visit by Indian Prime Minister Behari Vajpayee to Lahore on February 20–21 to inaugurate a Delhi-Lahore bus service. At the Martyrs Memorial there, Vajpayee affirmed India's support for the sovereignty of Pakistan.

The Lahore visit produced three agreements. First was the Lahore Declaration, which condemned terrorism and committed both countries to combating it. Second was a joint undertaking to refrain from intervention in each other's internal affairs. Third, and most important, was a memorandum of understanding (MOU) in which the two countries pledged to promote peace and stability through regular bilateral consultations, advance notification of ballistic missile tests, and steps to reduce the risk of accidental or unauthorized use of nuclear weapons.

The process suffered a setback within three months. In May, India discovered a major infiltration in the remote Kargil sector of Jammu and Kashmir province, an area adjoining China that had previously seen little conflict. The initial assessment was that the infiltrators were largely foreign mercenaries supported by the Pakistani military. Later, Indian intelligence suggested that almost all the infiltrators were Pakistani regulars from four battalions of the Northern Light Infantry. Six weeks of intense, though localized, conventional conflict ensued, including hand-to-hand combat at altitudes of over 16,000 feet, supported by heavy artillery bombardment by both sides. Artillery duels took place along much of the 740-kilometer Line of Control in Jammu and Kashmir. The intrusion was repelled, but at a heavy price, in part because the Indian government forbade its forces to cross into Pakistan despite the military advantages of doing so. Indian casualties were 469 dead and about 3,000 wounded.

The effects of the Kargil conflict are likely to be felt for some time. Vajpayee had invested considerable political capital in normalizing relations with Pakistan, and the conflict was a major embarrassment to him. It was India's first television war and it received saturation media coverage, often depicting the story in terms of good versus evil, accompanied by references to Indian mythology. The conflict also coincided with the Indian elections and was therefore highly politicized as candidates sought to gain maximum political mileage from the resulting patriotic fervor.

Moreover, in Pakistan, a series of events following the Kargil episode culminated in a military coup on October 12. Improvement in relations between the two countries seems unlikely as long as the Pakistani military continues to govern. India has now linked a resumption of dialogue to Pakistan's abjuring cross-border terrorism and ending hostile propaganda, conditions that Pakistan's new military rulers are unlikely to meet in the near future. In late 1999, cross-border skirmishes resumed. The hijacking of an Indian airliner on Christmas Eve, by what Indian authorities believe were Pakistani terrorists, further aggravated relations.

Meanwhile, the underlying Jammu and Kashmir problem is no nearer to solution. Throughout 1999, the level of insurgent actions in the province stayed high. India claims that 3,000 militants, mostly foreign mercenaries, have been eliminated in the last three years. Over 6,500 have been arrested in the same period. Additional Indian army troops were deployed in the province after the Kargil conflict. Troop strength has been doubled in Kargil, and another corps headquarters has been established to coordinate operations in the mountain region opposite China and Pakistan.

Relations with Other Neighbors. Developments to India's north-west, particularly in Afghanistan, are also troubling. Despite the successes of the Taliban, the group has not achieved full military victory in Afghanistan and hence is not recognized by India. Meanwhile, violence, terrorism, and narcotics trafficking remain major security issues.

New Delhi's engagement with the Central Asian republics of the former Soviet Union is based on a common interest in countering religious extremism, terrorism, and ethnic conflicts. India has participated in regional security initiatives, such as the Conference on Interaction and Confidence Building in Asia initiated by Kazakhstan, and working-level exchanges in military training and technical cooperation with the Central Asian nations.

India's relations with its other neighbors continue to be cordial. The king of Nepal was the chief guest at the Indian Republic Day celebrations in New Delhi in January 1999. India's vice-chief of army staff visited Sri Lanka for the fiftieth anniversary of the Sri Lankan Armed Forces. India continues to provide considerable military support to Bhutan and the Maldives. New Delhi maintains a dialogue with Myanmar on such issues of mutual security interest as border management and drug trafficking.

Relations with Southeast Asia. New Delhi continues its cooperative engagement of Southeast Asia. As a full dialogue partner of the Association of Southeast Asian Nations (ASEAN) and a member of the ASEAN Regional Forum (ARF), India is now more closely involved in promoting regional security. New Delhi seeks to develop mutually beneficial defense linkages with all countries of Southeast Asia and East Asia. Cooperation envisaged includes ship visits, training of service personnel, repair facilities for military equipment, supplies of spare parts, and joint development of equipment and technologies. In practice, however, little has happened.

Relations with the United States. India's military relationship with the United States is limited. Normal defense ties have not resumed since they were cut off following India's 1998 nuclear tests. Former mechanisms such as the annual meetings of the Defense Policy Group, the Joint Technical Group, and service-to-service steering groups continue to be suspended. Instead, there has been high-level strategic dialogue, the first of this intensity and duration between the two largest democracies in the world, conducted by U.S. Deputy Secretary of State Strobe Talbott and Indian Foreign Minister Jaswant Singh. Although no breakthroughs have been made, and none were expected, these discussions have led to a better understanding of each other's strategic concerns and interests.

INTERNAL ENVIRONMENT *Civil-Military Relations.* Harmonious civil-military relations have been a hallmark of Indian democracy over fifty years of independence. Relations suffered a severe blow on December 30, 1998, however, when the naval chief of staff was sacked without notice, a day after he assumed additional duties as chairman of the Joint Chiefs of Staff, the most senior military position in the nation. As the nominal commander in chief of the armed forces, the Indian president, with the direction of the cabinet, has the constitutional right to fire military heads. But the surreptitious manner in which this decision was made left the government open to criticism. The combative ex-chief and his spouse protested the firing through the media, widening the controversy. The episode was subsequently eclipsed by the Kargil conflict, but it could well return to affect future civil-military relations and therefore internal stability.

Ethnicity and Insurgency. India continues to face the challenge of maintaining a multiethnic society with a democratic political system. The rise of religious extremism on its borders and the global trend of ethnic assertiveness have not helped this cause. There are active insurgencies in four of the seven provinces in India's northeast. Violent Marxist communist movements continue in the eastern state of Bihar and the central province of Andhra Pradesh. And there is always the potential for spillover of the Tamil insurgency in Sri Lanka into India's southern Tamil Nadu province. India continues to deal with these problems within the civilian administrative structure and the police forces.

Nonmilitary Challenges to Security. India is increasingly aware of nontraditional and nonmilitary threats to its security. These threats include drug trafficking, money laundering, and narco-terrorism. Environmental security and sustainable development are other issues that must be addressed.

Ultimately the key to meeting many of these challenges is basic good governance. The elements of good governance include decentralization of executive authority, accountability in administration, delivery of development, and meeting minimum human needs. The Indian government is keenly aware of this, but its ability to deliver is not assured. The coming years will test its skill in addressing these issues while simultaneously meeting the needs of conventional and nuclear defense capabilities.

Finally, energy is critical to India's security in two major ways. First is India's continued dependence on imported oil for up to 60 percent of its total requirement. The other is India's close proximity to the rich energy resources of West Asia and Central Asia; conflicts over these resources could easily cross the border into India. To deal with these problems, India needs both to increase its use of renewable energy sources, such as hydropower and wind, and to develop infrastructure and arrangements for stable supplies of natural gas and oil from countries in West Asia and Central Asia.

DEFENSE POLICIES AND ISSUES

DRAFT NUCLEAR DOCTRINE   The major development in Indian defense policy in 1999 was the elaboration of one of its long-standing, fundamental security objectives: maintaining a secure and effective deterrent against the use or threat of use of weapons of mass destruction against India. The 1998 nuclear tests necessitated the articulation of a doctrine on the purpose and use of India's nuclear capability. Officials referred to the concept of "minimum deterrence" but did not spell it out in detail.

The first step toward defining this policy was the release on August 17, 1999, of a draft paper on Indian Nuclear Doctrine prepared by the government's National Security Advisory Board. As this occurred when the government was in caretaker status during the election period, the draft paper was thought by some to be a campaign gimmick. The government justified release of the document by arguing that public discussion and debate were necessary in the interest of national security.

The proposed nuclear doctrine was termed one of "minimum credible deterrence." Conceding that weapons of mass destruction constitute the gravest threat to international security, the paper argues that in the absence of any movement toward global nuclear disarmament, India has no alternative but to acquire such a capability. However, India would renounce first use of nuclear weapons, and would only strike in retaliation, exercising the right of self-defense. Further, India would not use or threaten use of nuclear weapons against states that do not possess nuclear weapons.

The proposed doctrine was a reflection of the general thinking of the government, but among security analysts there was concern over several issues. The paper visualizes a credible deterrent force as consisting of a triad of aircraft, mobile land-based missiles, and sea-based assets—comparable to the approach of the nuclear-capable countries in the 1960s. It, however, makes no attempt to specify the size of the stockpile, or the time frame, or the financial and physical requirements for acquiring nuclear capability. The only step made toward developing a nuclear delivery system since the 1998 tests has been a successful test in April 1999 of the 2,500-kilometer medium-range Agni II ballistic missile. Another unanswered question is the response of Pakistan and China to the doctrine, and the potential of an arms race in the region.

The initial euphoria following the nuclear tests quickly dissipated. Any serious antinuclear movement, however, was retarded by two intervening events. One was the Kargil conflict and the wave of nationalistic fervor it brought on. The other was the unilateral air campaign over Kosovo against the Serbs by the North Atlantic Treaty Organization, which raised the question of whether Serbia would have been attacked had it possessed nuclear weapons.

Thus, India enters the year 2000 with an embryonic nuclear capability and doctrine, but with many questions about its future nuclear policies.

INTERNAL SECURITY   There is a growing acceptance that internal security is an integral part of national defense. The government is determined to take steps to create a riot-free and terrorism-free India, and toward this end it is adopting a policy of "zero tolerance" for terrorism. This position was not maintained, however, in the Christmas Eve hijacking. Under the threats of the hijackers, the government released three prisoners, a step that was widely condemned by the media.

Table 1. India's Defense Budget (in billions of current rupees)

	1996–1997	1997–1998	1998–1999	1999–2000
Army	158.73	183.68	227.91	252.64
Air Force	74.92	91.27	91.90	102.79
Navy	39.76	47.65	61.91	67.63
R&D	15.36	19.51	23.00	27.73
Defense Production	7.3	10.67	7.28	6.14
Total	295.05	352.78	412.00	456.94

SOURCE: Indian government budgets.

NOTE: The exchange rate when the 1999–2000 budget was presented in March 1999 was approximately Rs42.00 to US$1. The inflation rate hovered in the high single digits throughout 1996–1999.

THE DEFENSE BUDGET   India's defense spending has grown steadily over the last decade but remains only 2.6 percent of gross domestic product. However, the defense budget does not include pensions and much of the nuclear-related expenditures.

Due to increasing commitments both for border defense and internal insurgencies, large deficiencies continue to plague India's armed forces. The Kargil conflict identified major weaknesses in funding, leading to a supplementary budget request for an additional 12 percent in December 1999.

All services have large wish lists. Some items that might be acquired quickly are the following:

- Multibarrel rocket system
- Medium artillery guns (towed and self-propelled)
- Unmanned aerial vehicles
- Surveillance systems and gun-locating radar
- Diesel submarines
- Low-level naval surveillance helicopters
- Advanced jet trainers
- AWACS
- Replacement combat fighters, such as MiG 27s and 29s, Jaguars, and Su-30s.

Contributions to Regional and Global Security

REGIONAL SECURITY   India participates actively in the South Asian Association for Regional Cooperation (SAARC). However, it spoiled its record somewhat when it blocked the annual SAARC summit in November in Kathmandu, citing the military coup in Pakistan as the reason. New Delhi is increasingly engaged with Southeast Asia as a full dialogue partner in ASEAN and as a member of the ASEAN Regional Forum. Some progress is beginning to take shape under the BIMSTEC (Bangladesh-India-Myanmar-Sri Lanka-Thailand Economic Cooperation) arrangement that India initiated in 1997. India is also active in the Indian Ocean Rim Association for Regional Cooperation (IOR-ARC).

India has a substantial economic stake in the Persian Gulf region. Its annual bilateral trade is over US$10 billion and annual foreign exchange remittances from the region amount to more than US$4 billion. India is vitally interested in the Israel-Arab peace process and has supported the relevant UN resolutions.

India continues to conduct bilateral visits and exercises with a number of navies of the world, particularly of Southeast Asian countries. In 1999, it took part for the first time in the tri-service Blue Crane exercises with South Africa and other countries of the Southern Africa Development Community (SADC) forum. It continues to host the "Milan" naval shore activities meeting for littoral navies in the Andaman Islands.

ARMS CONTROL Even after acquiring nuclear weapons, India remains committed to global nuclear disarmament. It strongly supports a nuclear weapons convention that would prohibit the development, production, stockpiling, and use or threat of use of nuclear weapons and provide for the elimination of all existing weapons under international verification. India has committed not to conduct any further nuclear weapons tests. The government is working to develop a domestic consensus for signing the Comprehensive Test Ban Treaty, although given the deep differences on this subject, early progress is unlikely. India also supports negotiating a Fissile Material Cut-off Treaty at the Conference on Disarmament that would ban production of all fissile material for weapons purposes.

India ratified the Chemical Weapons Convention as an original state party. It is also a party to the Biological and Toxic Weapons Convention of 1972, and participates in the Ad Hoc Group in Geneva negotiating a protocol to the convention. In August 1999, India ratified the Amended Protocol II on Anti-personnel Landmines of the 1980 Treaty on Certain Conventional Weapons.

GLOBAL SECURITY India continues to remain actively engaged in UN peacekeeping operations. In November 1998, it provided a battalion group to the UN Interim Force in Lebanon (UNIFIL). A year later, another battalion replaced the initial force. In an MOU signed with the United Nations, India has committed a brigade to be available at short notice for peacekeeping operations.

8 Indonesia

The Security Environment

Indonesia entered the year 2000 with mixed prospects. On the one hand, the election of a new president, Abdurrahman Wahid, and vice-president, Megawati Sukarnoputri, in October 1999 brought hope for the birth of a new Indonesia. On the other hand, the new government faces the enormous challenge of stimulating economic recovery, restoring political stability, ending ongoing ethnic and religious conflicts, and even preserving the territorial integrity of the Indonesian state in the face of secessionism. Externally, the international community has come to view Indonesia—once considered a major actor in regional stability—as a source of instability.

INTERNAL ENVIRONMENT *Economic Uncertainty.* Macroeconomic conditions in Indonesia stabilized during the first and second quarters of 1999; gross domestic product rose 1.3 percent and 0.5 percent, respectively, versus a decline of 15 percent in 1998. Between March and September, the inflation index declined from 77.6 percent in 1998 to 0.02 percent. The rupiah strengthened against the U.S. dollar at the end of 1998, remained relatively stable at Rp8,600–8,700 per dollar into the second quarter of 1999, then strengthened further to Rp6,600 after the June national elections. Interest rates decreased from 30 percent in April and May to 13 percent in August.

However, economic conditions remained highly uncertain. The rupiah continued to fluctuate, and at the end of 1999 was at about Rp7,000 per dollar. Exports and imports, which grew significantly from January to May, declined again in June. Poverty, unemployment, street children, school drop-outs, and the prices of medicines and medical supplies all continued to increase. Attempts to remedy these problems were hampered by mismanagement of funds, including persistent government corruption.

Problems in the banking sector were primarily responsible for preventing recovery. Until July, the bank recapitalization program was strengthening market confidence in Indonesia. In mid-August, however, confidence evaporated when it was revealed that a company linked to President B. J. Habibie's Golkar party had collected Rp546 billion (US$76.9 million at US$1 = Rp7,000) in fees for helping Bank Bali obtain Rp904 billion (US$132.39 million) in government loan guarantees. The scandal led the International Monetary Fund (IMF), the World Bank, and the Asian Development Bank to suspend assistance to the country in September.

As the Wahid government begins to unveil its program, there have been signs of improvement. The IMF and the World Bank pledged the resumption of financial assistance, and the government is working to rebuild the country's confidence, especially from the economically important Chinese Indonesian community. Nevertheless, restoring market confidence and implementing a sustained recovery program are major challenges.

Religious, Ethnic, and Urban Conflict. Social tensions continued and even intensified in some regions in 1999. The most intractable situation was religious conflict in Ambon, capital of Maluku province, which previously had been considered a model of interfaith relations. Early in the year, a petty criminal act by a group of youths triggered a devastating and prolonged outbreak of violence between Christians and Muslims. Hundreds died, thousands fled to other islands, and huge numbers of houses and shops were damaged or burned. The violence subsided in April but picked up again in August. As the year 2000 began, Maluku continued to undergo religious bloodletting, raising levels of tension elsewhere in the country.

An area of serious ethnic conflict was Sambas, in West Kalimantan province. The economic crisis exacerbated long-standing tensions between the indigenous Dayaks and Malays and more recent immigrants, who were mainly government-sponsored transmigrants from Madura Island in East Java province. A series of violent clashes left many people dead and many buildings destroyed; thousands of Madurese were suddenly refugees.

A wave of urban violence spread through Indonesia's major cities as well. The first half of 1999 saw numerous small-scale riots, mass brawls, and other incidents, which the security apparatus seemed unable to stop. This undermined people's confidence in the authorities—a situation that the new government has inherited.

Rebellious Regions. The concentration of power in the central government during Suharto's rule created a heavily unbalanced relationship between Jakarta and Indonesia's provinces, particularly in the outer islands. Secessionist movements were founded in East Timor, Aceh, and Irian Jaya. Harsh responses by the military suppressed these movements under Suharto, but since his downfall in May 1998, regional aspirations have been voiced more openly and forcefully.

Of the rebellious territories, only East Timor is on the road toward independence. In January 1999, President Habibie offered East Timor a referendum that would determine East Timor's autonomy within Indonesia or its independence. On May 5, Indonesia, Portugal, and the United Nations agreed that the United Nations would oversee the referendum, while Indonesia remained responsible for security. On August 30, a decisive 78.5 percent of East Timorese voted for independence.

Immediately after the result was announced on September 4, pro-Indonesian militias sponsored by Indonesia's military went on a rampage. Hundreds of thousands of East Timorese were forced to seek refuge in churches or to flee to the hills or the Indonesian-controlled West Timor. The campaign continued for days, destroying Dili and many other East Timorese communities. UN observers and others accused the Indonesian military of fomenting and participating in the violence.

The impact of the violence in East Timor was enormous, both domestically and internationally. Domestically, the situation was a demonstration of the military's failure to provide security, and it had the further effect of undoing Habibie's ambitions to retain the presidency. The tragedy also sent a strong message, whether intended or not, to other regions about the consequences of attempts at secession.

The message did not deter the Acehnese. Rather, it appeared to increase the determination of the Gerakan Aceh Merdeka, or GAM (Free Aceh Movement), the main armed group. Meanwhile, delays in prosecuting military officers responsible for human rights violations in Aceh fueled public sympathy for the independence movement. On November 8, more than a million people gathered in the provincial capital to demand a referendum on independence. This was a shock to the new Wahid government, which had been attempting to open a dialogue on autonomy.

Aceh poses a more serious threat to Indonesia's national integrity than did East Timor. Aceh is larger (4.2 million versus 800,000 in East Timor), but more importantly it was part of the Dutch East Indies, the basis for the Indonesian state, whereas East Timor was a Portuguese colony annexed in 1976. Other restive regions include Irian Jaya, Riau, Maluku, and South Sulawesi.

To restore internal stability, Jakarta must address grievances and demands for greater regional autonomy. The disintegration of Indonesia would also pose difficult security problems for the larger Asia Pacific region.

Political Developments. The nation's general election in June 1999, the first openly contested election since 1955, was peaceful and judged by observers as free and fair—representing a major step toward democratization. The election filled 462 of 500 seats in the national parliament (DPR, Dewan Perwakilan Rakyat), but no political party won enough seats to form a government (see table 1). This state of affairs produced intense maneuvering within the political elite for the selection of a president by the People's Consultative Assembly (MPR, Majelis Permusyawaratan Rakyat) in October. Historic divisions between Islamic and nationalist elements in Indonesian politics, coupled with factionalism within many of the parties, added to the uncertainty.

The principal competitors were a loose coalition of Islam-oriented parties, known as the "Central Axis," which nominated the respected Islamic leader and political activist Wahid, and more secular nationalist parties that supported Megawati of the Indonesian Democratic Party —Struggle (PDI-P), which finished first in the election. Habibie and his supporters in Golkar were left to maneuver between these groups. When

Table 1. The Results of General Elections, June 1999

Political Parties	Vote (%)	Seats in Parliament
Indonesian Democratic Party—Struggle (PDI-P)	33.7	153
Golkar Party	22.4	120
United Development Party (PPP)*	10.7	58
National Awakening Party (PKB)	12.6	51
National Mandate Party (PAN)*	7.1	34
Moon and Star Party (PBB)*	1.9	13
Others (smaller parties)	11.5	33

SOURCE: Based on official results from the Indonesian General Election Commission.
NOTE: Percentages do not total 100 because of rounding.
* "Central Axis" members

the MPR rejected Habibie's accountability speech on October 19, Habibie withdrew his candidacy, and a reform-oriented faction within Golkar then threw its support to Wahid, which led to Wahid's victory over Megawati in a very close vote. Wahid then supported Megawati for the vice-presidency, thus defusing the tension in the air.

The cohesiveness and effectiveness of the new government remains to be seen. Wahid and Megawati are long-standing friends, which facilitates their working relationship. Wahid, however, had initially supported Megawati's candidacy before pursuing his own, and this may have left bitterness in Megawati's camp. Further, in the interest of stability, Wahid appointed a "national unity" cabinet representing all major parties including Golkar. Some members have divided loyalties, and in some appointments political considerations outweigh expertise. Also worrisome from the perspective of building a stable democratic process is the lack of an organized opposition.

Role of the Military. The position and the future role of the military pose another uncertainty. Ever since the resignation of Suharto, the military has been politically weakened and on the defensive. In an encouraging step toward civilian governance, a civilian was appointed as minister of defense for the first time. Also, for the first time since 1965 a navy rather than army officer holds the position of commander in chief of the armed forces.

But the military's withdrawal from Indonesian politics is not yet in sight. The military is still Indonesia's single most powerful institution, and it holds thirty-eight appointed seats in the parliament. Wahid appointed generals to four important cabinet positions, including coordinating minister for security and political affairs and the minister for home affairs. It is also likely that the government will have to call on the military to help restore order and maintain national unity in times of difficulty.

There were increasing signs of tension in civilian-military relations as 1999 ended, centering on the military's role in the East Timor violence. As a commission established by Indonesia's National Commission for Human Rights tentatively concluded, "The military leadership knew what was happening but chose not to do anything to prevent it." The military leadership denied this allegation, and new Defense Minister Juwono Sudarsono warned that pushing the military further on this subject might backfire. There were also reports of cooling relations between President Wahid and Coordinating Minister (and former commander in chief and defense minister) General Wiranto that reached a crescendo early in the new year. The role of the military and its relationship to civilian authority remains one of the critical issues for Indonesia in the years ahead.

EXTERNAL ENVIRONMENT *Regional Developments.* Indonesia's perception of the regional security environment has not changed significantly over the last year. The Asian financial crisis reinforced the view that economic security is a crucial element of regional resilience. The crisis also underscored the strategic importance of outside forces, such as the IMF, the World Bank, and the United States.

Nevertheless, among the elite and within society, dependence on external help generates insecurity and suspicion of the outside world. Some believe that there has been foreign involvement in the unrest in Indonesia's regions, including support for the GAM by neighboring countries, and that Western countries, especially the United States, have a grand design to dismember Indonesia.

Despite greater democratization, Indonesia's government is sensitive over perceived foreign interference in its domestic affairs. The Indonesian government, like most members of the Association of Southeast Asian Nations (ASEAN), sees U.S. promotion of democracy and human rights as patronizing, intrusive, and contrary to ASEAN's principle of noninterference. The suggestion by some ASEAN members that the organization reconsider this noninterference principle has only exacerbated this sense of insecurity; Indonesia rejected this proposal at the ASEAN Ministerial Meeting in Singapore in July 1999.

Indonesia's domestic crisis has also impacted intra-ASEAN relations and raised regional concerns. Economic hardship has increased the number of illegal migrants to neighboring countries, Malaysia in particular, and this has been the cause of bilateral friction. Nonconventional security problems, such as the 1997 forest fires in Indonesia that affected neighboring states, could become contentious again, especially while Indonesia continues to be preoccupied with domestic problems.

Renewed Activism. The new government fully recognizes these problems. Shortly after his election, President Wahid traveled to all ASEAN member countries, with the exception of Brunei, to reassure the governments of Jakarta's commitment to good relations. This tour, followed by visits to the United States and Japan, signaled the return of an activist Indonesian foreign policy as well as the desire to regain standing as a respected member of the international community. Wahid also announced that Indonesia would be "equidistant," placing emphasis on its relations with Asian countries including China and India. Still more controversially, Wahid announced a plan to open direct trade relations with Israel. These two initiatives, if implemented, would constitute significant shifts in Indonesia's foreign policy.

East Timor and Relations with Australia. The East Timor tragedy and the resulting international outrage dramatically changed Indonesia's relations with the West. Several Western countries, with Australia at the forefront, put strong pressure on Indonesia to restore order or accept international intervention. Increasingly isolated, Habibie on September 12 reluctantly accepted a UN-approved, Australian-led International Force in East Timor (INTERFET).

Jakarta's decision sparked domestic uproar, with almost daily protests and demonstrations. The strongest anger was directed against Australia, previously seen as a friend. The Habibie government canceled a 1995 security treaty with Australia and postponed sending a new ambassador to Canberra. Calls for a break in diplomatic ties with Canberra escalated after incidents between INTERFET and Indonesian forces occurred along the West/East Timor border. An interview, in which Australian Prime Minister John Howard suggested that Australia was "a deputy for the United States," appeared to confirm suspicion that Canberra was exploiting the crisis to expand its position in the region. Indeed, many Indonesians, rightly or wrongly, now view Australia as the greatest threat to Indonesia's national pride, security, and territorial unity.

Strained Indonesian-Australian relations, including the risk of military confrontation, complicate efforts to build a stable and peaceful regional order. But there are no signs that the Wahid government will take early steps to restore a more positive relationship. President Wahid has reportedly said that significant improvements will only be possible once Australia has a new government. Nevertheless, by the end of 1999, open anti-Australian sentiment had subsided. If this trend continues, normalized relations are only a matter of time.

DEFENSE POLICIES AND ISSUES

STRATEGIC PRIORITIES Indonesia's defense strategy remains defensive and internally focused. The military faces the major challenge of maintaining domestic stability and order at a time of extreme political uncertainty. But with a damaged reputation and growing popular opposition to the military's political role, internal consolidation and image rebuilding have gained priority. A number of steps have been taken toward this objective. They include acceptance of a reduction from seventy-five to thirty-eight appointed seats in parliament, separation of the police from the armed forces, a deliberate display of neutrality during the June elections, and even a change of name from Indonesian Armed Forces (ABRI, Angkatan Bersenjata Republik Indonesia) to Indonesian National Military (TNI, Tentara Nasional Indonesia) in April. However, there is still a long way to go to restore the public trust.

One major shift in strategic priorities may be taking place under the Wahid government. For the first time since 1957, Indonesia has begun to pay more attention to its status as a maritime state. This is seen in the appointment of a navy officer as armed forces commander in chief and in the creation of a new Ministry for Maritime Exploration. There are unconfirmed reports that the navy and TNI are preparing a major review of current defense doctrine.

SPENDING AND PROCUREMENT   The severe effects of the economic crisis continue to affect the military budget. No new major purchases were made during 1999. In July, however, Indonesia's navy launched a US$10.6 million project with South Korea to build a search-and-rescue ship. The East Timor crisis also affected procurement. In mid-September, the last three of sixteen British Aerospace Hawk 100/200 jets ordered in 1993 were held in Bangkok while en route to Jakarta, apparently due to an EU decision to suspend military assistance to Indonesia. (The jets were later delivered.)

At the end of November, Defense Minister Juwono asked parliament for a 62.9 percent increase in the defense budget, from Rp11.6 trillion (US$1.63 billion) in 1999 to Rp18.9 trillion (US$ 2.66 billion). The request was based on the need to ensure that the military becomes more professional and financially independent. The largest segment, around Rp9.12 trillion (US$1.28 billion), is earmarked for equipment and arms procurement, with Rp5.45 trillion (US$767.6 million) for salaries. The allocation between the services was not specified, but there is speculation that, despite President Wahid's interest in developing naval capabilities, the much larger army would have higher priority.

DEFENSE COOPERATION AND CONFLICT   Before the East Timor events, Indonesia's defense cooperation activities proceeded normally.

From July 26 to August 15, Indonesia joined New Zealand, the Philippines, Singapore, and Papua New Guinea in Fleet Concentration Period Kakadu-4/99, a military exercise in Darwin organized by Australia. At the end of August, Indonesia's navy conducted bilateral exercises with the United States, CARAT-V/99 (Cooperation Afloat Readiness and Training), in Surabaya and Situbondo, East Java. Even after the East Timor crisis, on October 12, Indonesia's navy signed an agreement with its Singapore counterpart formally establishing a joint military training facility in Kayu Ara Island, Riau province.

However, the East Timor turmoil seriously affected Indonesia's defense cooperation with Australia and the United States. Both countries suspended military ties with Indonesia. The suspension is likely to continue as long as the situation in East Timor remains volatile and until the question of alleged human rights violations by Indonesian military personnel is properly addressed. Nevertheless, under the Wahid government, the prospects for progress, especially with the United States, seem improved.

CONTRIBUTIONS TO REGIONAL AND GLOBAL SECURITY

Despite its own security problems, Indonesia continues to contribute to both regional and global security, especially in nontraditional ways. It has been active in countering smuggling and illegal exploitation of marine resources. In January and February, Indonesia arrested some 140 foreign vessels for fishing illegally in its maritime jurisdiction. In May and June, the air force participated in fighting forest fires in Kalimantan.

Antipiracy is another area of activity, especially in the Strait of Malacca where incidents have increased since the economic crisis. In April, Indonesia set up a special Monitoring Command center and stationed an Antipiracy Unit on Batam Island, stepping up joint patrols with Singapore. The early success of this effort was indicated by no reports of piracy during July–August. This is a modest achievement, but significant given the international importance of the Strait of Malacca.

Indonesia's conventional contributions to regional security during 1999 were more problematic. On the one hand, Indonesia continued to participate in ASEAN and other regional institutions, including the ASEAN Regional Forum. On the other hand, its domestic security problems and the violence in East Timor, Aceh, and elsewhere were sources of instability.

Indonesia's contributions to global security have been meager, though consistent. Indonesia continues to support efforts toward global disarmament and arms control, nuclear nonproliferation, and elimination of weapons of mass destruction. Indonesia also supports the international role of the United Nations.

But since the East Timor turmoil, the international community has viewed Indonesia almost as a pariah state. This was manifested in the UN Commission on Human Rights vote on September 27 to establish an inquiry into allegations of atrocities in East Timor. Compromise language in the resolution, however, allows Indonesian and international investigators to cooperate, thus saving Indonesia from the ostracism of Rwanda and Yugoslavia. Indonesia has the opportunity to restore its dignity, rehabilitate its tainted image, and regain its standing as a responsible member of the international community.

9 Japan

THE SECURITY ENVIRONMENT

Japan enters the twenty-first century with its basic defense policies intact, but with respect to its future security needs, it faces uncertainty. Relations with China and North Korea are worrisome, and a growing number of Japanese argue that Japan must rely on itself rather than count on its alliance with the United States to meet new defense challenges. While Japanese were relieved that economic growth revived in much of Asia in 1999, the Japanese economy managed only weak growth, and this was due to government stimulus programs that accumulated massive debt. Thus, Japan finds significant risks both in its external physical security environment and in its human security at home.

DOMESTIC DEVELOPMENTS   Prime Minister Obuchi Keizō has shown surprising political strength despite the continued weakness of the economy. Initially, when he assumed office in July 1998, it was expected that Obuchi would prove to be yet another in a string of largely ineffective and short-lived prime ministers. Obuchi's Liberal Democratic Party (LDP) held a majority of seats in the House of Representatives (Lower House) but not in the House of Councillors (Upper House). While the government made headway on some important economic proposals, controversial defense bills remained deadlocked.

In January 1999, Obuchi strengthened the LDP's position by forming a coalition with the Liberal Party, facilitating passage of the security bills. He subsequently expanded the coalition to include the New Kōmeitō (Clean Government Party), giving the government a majority in the Upper House. As a result, in the 145th ordinary Diet session, the

94

Obuchi government passed nearly 90 percent of the government's proposed legislation. This included bills, passed in August, legitimating the national flag and national anthem.

While the coalition government and Obuchi's September reelection as LDP president (hence, prime minister) have given Japan political stability, defense policy is still controversial. The most serious policy matter of 1999 occurred shortly after the inauguration of the new Obuchi cabinet in October. Obuchi had appointed Nishimura Shingo, a Liberal Party member known for his provocative, hawkish views, as a parliamentary vice-minister for defense. Inexperienced in a cabinet position, Nishimura suggested that the Diet should discuss the possibility of Japan's possessing nuclear weapons. Opposition parties immediately seized on this statement as contrary to the Three Non-Nuclear Principles, and Obuchi was forced to replace Nishimura. Although the incident blew over quickly, it demonstrated the continuing polarization of views on core security questions even within conservative ruling groups. Among younger conservatives, there emerged as well a willingness to debate issues long considered taboo.

Other events in 1999 included a serious radiation accident, caused by careless operating practices, at the Tōkaimura Nuclear Facility in Ibaraki prefecture in late September. One of the workers exposed to the radiation later died. Moreover, the government's crisis management response was slow and considered by many as inadequate.

In October, scandal surrounded the defense procurement headquarters of the Japan Defense Agency (JDA) over the issue of prearranged bidding for fuel procurement. In 1998, charges of bribery and breaches of trust in the procurement office had led to the resignation of the defense minister, reorganization of the procurement office, and conviction of the office's former director-general for bribery. The new scandal tarnished the JDA's reputation further.

Most important for the future Obuchi government's survival, however, is economic recovery. The government's economic stimulus packages began to take hold in 1999, lifting the economy toward positive, though still anemic, growth. Company restructuring and merger and acquisition activity were at unprecedented levels for Japan, resulting in historically high unemployment but also offering promise of productivity growth in the future. Yet, major problems have not gone away. Japanese banks still have serious debt problems, and consumer spending and corporate domestic investment remain depressed. A high yen during the latter part of 1999 hindered export expansion, traditionally Japan's formula for overcoming recession. Deficit spending grew, raising Japan's debt level to well over 100 percent of gross domestic product, the highest in the industrialized world. Concern within the bureaucracy has grown, but a reverse in policy direction toward fiscal retrenchment could cut off what little growth the economy has managed to achieve.

THE EXTERNAL ENVIRONMENT   The Japanese government's strong support of the U.S.-Japan security relationship is based on the belief that the alliance remains essential to regional stability in an uncertain and changing security environment. From the Japanese perspective, two tension spots, the Korean peninsula and the Taiwan Strait, are directly related to Japan's own security. Moreover, Japan's main sea lines of communication with the Middle East and Europe pass through the South China Sea, where there are multiple overlapping territorial claims, and the straits connecting the South China Sea with the Indian Ocean. Aside these vital waterways sits politically fragile Indonesia, with its deep social fissures accentuated by economic crisis. These challenges have heightened debate within Japan about basic security approaches.

North Korea. North Korea's provocations and brinkmanship are deeply troubling for Japan, although developments toward the end of 1999 gave some hope for a diplomatic modus vivendi. Japan's defense white paper for 1999 emphasized Tokyo's primary concern with North Korea's offensive capabilities, especially its nuclear potential and its ongoing missile development program. Pyongyang's August 1998 launching of a missile (as Japan believes) or satellite (as North Korea claims) over Japanese territory had a major impact on the Japanese security debate. The launch demonstrated North Korea's capability to spread any conflict on the peninsula to adjacent countries. The Japanese government responded quickly, determining that it should develop its own reconnaissance satellites, a proposal endorsed by U.S. Defense Secretary William Cohen in March 1999.

In another incident, the Japanese government in March 1999 authorized the Maritime Self-Defense Force (MSDF) to engage two ships that had ignored orders to stop in Japanese territorial waters. This was the first such order since the Self-Defense Forces (SDF) was established in 1954. The ships escaped into North Korean waters. On April 5, then Chief Cabinet Secretary Nonaka Hiromu testified before a Diet special committee that the government would reexamine procedures to ensure prompt authorization of security operations and use of weapons under similar circumstances in the future.

On the positive side, the threat of North Korean missiles produced a relatively high degree of common resolve on the part of the Japanese, South Korean, and U.S. governments in particular and the international community in general. The Group of Eight (G-8), at Japan's urging, warned Pyongyang in late June against a second missile launch. Similar warnings came from a bilateral discussion between South Korean President Kim Dae Jung and U.S. President Bill Clinton in early July and a Kim-Obuchi meeting in early September. In mid-September, a breakthrough was achieved in Berlin by U.S. and North Korean negotiators, averting another missile launch. In return, the Japanese government joined the U.S. government in easing economic sanctions against Pyongyang. In December, Nonaka and former Prime Minister Murayama Tomiichi visited Pyongyang, the first official visit at this level since 1990, to promote the normalization of diplomatic relations. The Japanese agenda included the missile question and suspected kidnappings of several Japanese citizens by North Korea.

China, Taiwan, and TMD. The relationship between China and Taiwan is a major Japanese concern. In early July, Taiwan leader Lee Teng-hui surprised the world, including Japan, by declaring China and Taiwan as having the character of a "special state–to-state relationship." Beijing predictably reacted strongly. Shortly afterwards (and probably in reaction to U.S. accusations of Chinese espionage in the United States), Beijing announced its possession of neutron bomb technology; in August, Beijing announced it had launched a new intercontinental ballistic missile (ICBM). These developments increased Taipei's desire to promote and participate in the development of a theater missile defense (TMD) system. Such China-Taiwan tensions are especially sensitive for Japan because the question of whether Taiwan contingencies are included among "situations in areas surrounding Japan which have significant importance to the security of Japan" is a central issue in the new Guidelines for U.S.-Japan Defense Cooperation.

In mid-August, after several years of discussions, the U.S.-Japan agreement on TMD was formalized in a memorandum of understanding (MOU). The two parties agreed to begin joint research on Navy Theater Wide Defense (NTWD), a mobile, sea-based system to be carried on Aegis ships. However, China's vehement opposition to TMD remains a significant problem, and the TMD issue has become one of the most controversial security issues in Northeast Asia.

U.S.-Japan Security Relations. According to a mid-December Yomiuri-Gallup public opinion survey, 77 percent of Japanese believe that if Japan were attacked, the United States would help, and 67 percent of Americans think that the United States should help Japan. Eighty-four percent of Japanese and 73 percent of Americans believe that the two countries will be good partners in the twenty-first century. On other issues, however, there are more significant differences in perception. For example, 51 percent of Americans but only 25 percent of Japanese see a potential military threat from China.

DEFENSE POLICIES AND ISSUES

GUIDELINES FOR DEFENSE COOPERATION There are three laws implementing the Guidelines for U.S.-Japan Defense Cooperation: the act on sustaining the peace and security of Japan in "situations in areas surrounding Japan," the revised Self-Defense Forces Law, and the revised Acquisition and Cross-Servicing Agreement (ACSA). The bills had been submitted to the Diet in April 1998, but were hung up for a year due to a stalemate in the Lower House and a setback for the LDP in the 1998 Upper House election. In 1999, the bills were passed by the Lower House on April 27 and the Upper House on May 24.

The revision of the SDF Law allows the SDF to dispatch ships and aircraft to rescue Japanese citizens overseas in cases of emergency; the original SDF Law allowed only the dispatch of airplanes. The revision of the ACSA permits supplying U.S. forces not only in peacetime but also in situations in areas surrounding Japan that are important to Japan's peace and security.

The act on "situations in areas surrounding Japan" contains three major provisions:

(1) The SDF may provide rear area support to U.S. forces, search and rescue, and inspection of suspicious ships on the high seas;

(2) The Japanese government may request that local government bodies and the private sector cooperate with the central government and U.S. forces; and

(3) The SDF may use weapons when necessary.

Opposition parties and even the Liberal Party of Ozawa Ichirō had raised questions in the Diet on the bill regarding "situations in areas surrounding Japan," which led to changes in the final bill of the government. The main issues, and the government response, were as follows:

(1) Should the bill make clear that it comes within the framework

of the U.S.-Japan Security Treaty? The final bill states that it *is* within the framework of the treaty.

(2) What is the definition of "situations in areas surrounding Japan"? The concept is not geographical but situational; included in the final bill is the qualification: "for example, cases which may develop into a direct military attack on Japan if let alone."

(3) Do plans for action by the SDF require advance approval by the Diet? Diet approval is required in principle, but in emergencies approval can be retroactive.

(4) Is it possible to distinguish clearly between combat area and rear area (in which case the SDF would provide logistic support to U.S. forces in an action)? The newly established Constitutional Research Commission of the Diet will discuss the question together with the concept of collective self-defense.

(5) Is a UN Security Council resolution required for the SDF to inspect suspicious ships on the high seas? The question remains; in the final bill, ship inspection is not addressed (and will be dealt with by future legislation), because of strong Liberal Party opposition to the requirement of a resolution.

(6) How specific must the government be in requests to local governing bodies and the private sector for their cooperation with U.S. forces? On this question the government sought to demonstrate the degree of specificity by providing ten examples.

In the final votes, the three coalition parties supported all three bills. The Democratic Party supported the revisions of the SDF Law and the ACSA, but opposed the bill on sustaining peace in areas surrounding Japan. The Japan Communist Party and the Social Democratic Party opposed all three bills.

DEFENSE BUDGET   On December 25, 1998, the cabinet approved the budget for the 1999 fiscal year. The total was ¥81,860.1 billion (US$799 billion at US$1 = ¥102.4), an increase of 5.4 percent over the previous year. The defense budget was ¥4,932.2 billion (US$48.05 billion), representing a decrease of 0.2 percent from 1998 in a second consecutive year of decreased defense spending. An additional ¥12.1 billion (US$118.16 million) was budgeted for relocation of certain U.S. military facilities on Okinawa under the Special Action Committee on Okinawa. The defense budget accounted for 6 percent of the total budget and 0.991 percent of GDP.

Of the 1999 defense budget, 44 percent was allocated to personnel and provisions, 17 percent to equipment and materials, and 39 percent to logistical support. Allocation among the three services was as follows: Ground Self-Defense Force 44.9 percent, MSDF 27.8 percent, and Air Self-Defense Force 27.3 percent.

The total amount for equipment and materials was ¥796.5 billion (US$7.78 billion), a decrease of 0.2 percent from the previous year. The research and development budget was ¥130.7 billion (US$1.27 billion) and base security and support for U.S. forces in Japan ¥540.2 billion (US$5.28 billion), increases of 2.4 percent and 3.8 percent respectively from the previous year. Due to the North Korean missile issue, the budgets for TMD development and radar enhancements were almost fully approved. In addition, due to the defense procurement scandal, ¥2.5 million (US$24,414) was approved for reorganizing defense procurement.

The budget passed the Diet on March 17. (The opposition majority in the Upper House rejected the bill, but the constitution gives the Lower House supremacy in budget matters.)

PROCUREMENT   Of the targets set in the Mid-term Defense Program for 1996–2000, procurement under the 1999 budget should have achieved 78 percent of the goal for Type-90 tanks, 86 percent for destroyers, 80 percent for submarines, 100 percent for F-15 fighters, and 80 percent for F-2 fighter-support aircraft.

OKINAWA   In June, U.S. President Clinton expressed hope that the problem of relocating U.S. military bases in Okinawa would be resolved by the next G-8 summit, to be held in Okinawa in July 2000. His remarks, which appeared to set a deadline, caused complications between the Japanese central government and the Okinawa prefectural government. In April, the Obuchi cabinet officially determined that the summit would take place in Nago, Okinawa.

In August, Okinawa Governor Inamine Keiichi visited Tokyo to lobby for a plan whereby the government would utilize the land occupied by the U.S. Marine Corps' Futenma Air Station. In early September, the central and prefectural governments began final negotiations to relocate the Futenma base to Nago. Governor Inamine asked that use of the new base by U.S. forces be limited to fifteen years, a condition the United States will not accept. In late December, the Nago city assembly passed a resolution accepting a new heliport base. Thus, the Futenma relocation issue appears finally to be on the way to solution, but the longer-term future of U.S. installations in Okinawa remains a potent political issue.

CONTRIBUTIONS TO REGIONAL AND GLOBAL SECURITY

NORTHEAST ASIA   In May, the Japanese government signed an agreement to provide US$1 billion of the total US$4.6 billion cost of developing light water reactors in North Korea through the Korean Peninsula Energy Development Organization (KEDO). In July, all political parties in the Diet approved this decision. In August, the first joint search-and-rescue training exercise between the MSDF and the South Korean Navy was conducted in the East China Sea. At the second Ministerial Round-Table in late October, Japan and South Korea agreed to cooperate further with the United States in dealing with North Korea and to expand cultural exchanges with each other. In late December, Japanese and North Korean Red Cross missions met in Beijing and agreed on the early resumption of Japanese food assistance to North Korea.

The Japanese government also continued its security dialogue with China in a regular meeting in early October. However, the two sides remained apart over the issue of Taiwan, expressing concern about each other's defense policies.

DEVELOPMENT ASSISTANCE   Japan's Official Development Assistance (ODA) was US$10.8 billion in 1998, an increase of 14 percent over the previous year; in response to the financial crisis, the allocation of ODA for Asia increased to 61 percent of the total from 47 percent the previous year. In August 1999, the government released a midterm ODA plan. The plan declared no quantitative goal, but it stated that ODA should be flexibly utilized and should be linked to Japanese national interests and foreign policies. By some measures, Japan is the largest donor of bilateral ODA in the world, but the quality of its ODA is frequently criticized at home and abroad. However, the special Miyazawa Fund is making a major contribution toward helping in the economic recovery of developing Asian countries.

THE UN AND PEACEKEEPING   In April 1999, the Japanese government agreed to provide US$200 million for refugees in Kosovo; in August, it sent two foreign ministry officials to Kosovo to participate in the UN activities. In July, the government extended SDF participation in the UN Disengagement Observer Force on the Golan Heights, and it sent three police to East Timor as part of a civilian police organization under UN authority. In September, after the UN Security Council resolution authorizing a multinational force for East Timor, Tokyo provided US$2 million to the UN High Commissioner for Refugees for its work in East Timor.

In late August, four Japanese mining engineers working for the Japan International Cooperation Agency in the Kyrgyz Republic were taken hostage by an armed Islamic group. The four engineers were finally released in late October, but the incident raised questions about the security of Japanese citizens working abroad for international organizations. The Japanese government denied that it paid a ransom to the terrorists, but the rumor persisted.

Assignment of SDF members to core units of UN peacekeeping forces —for such purposes as stationing and patrol in buffer zones—is currently frozen. Under its International Peace Cooperation Law, Japan has five principles that strictly govern its contributions to peacekeeping forces:

(1) The parties in conflict shall have agreed on a cease-fire;

(2) The parties, including the territorial state(s), shall have agreed to the peacekeeping force and to Japan's participation;

(3) The peacekeeping force shall maintain strict impartiality;

(4) Japan may withdraw if any of these requirements ceases to be met; and

(5) Use of weapons shall be limited to the minimum required to protect the lives of the Japanese mission members.

In August, however, the LDP and the New Kōmeitō reached agreement that the SDF should be assigned to core units of peacekeeping forces. This could well lead to revision of the law.

10 Republic of Korea

A half century after the outbreak of the Korean War, there are still two antagonistic Korean states and nearly a million men in arms ranged along their common border. This situation, punctuated by periodic incidents such as the brief naval engagements in mid-1999, has been so much a part of daily life that South Koreans have learned to accept a considerable degree of military insecurity as a normal condition. At the same time, the underlying uncertainties make South Koreans acutely aware of developments that could affect the security of the Korean peninsula. The alleviation of tensions remains a governmental and a national priority. The current government, under Kim Dae Jung, seeks to accomplish this through a "Sunshine Policy" toward the North even as it strengthens relations with its immediate neighbors and continues to rely on the U.S. security guarantee. While no basic breakthrough has yet occurred in inter-Korean relations, South Koreans begin the new century with a sense of optimism. Relations with both Japan and China have improved, and Japan, the United States, and South Korea have strengthened policy coordination in dealing with North Korea. Also reassuring —and more immediately relevant to many South Koreans—the country is making a sharp recovery from the 1997–1998 economic crisis. There remain, however, many economic as well as political sources of insecurity.

INTERNAL ISSUES   There is no significant internal challenge to the South Korean state or to the basic political and economic values associated with that state, despite continued North Korean efforts to foment unrest. Few South Koreans fear a return to military-led government or other significant abridgement of political rights. From this perspective, the South Korean response to the economic crisis was quite reassuring. There was no retreat back toward statism or erosion of democratic governance. Indeed, the democratic election that brought Kim Dae Jung to the presidency occurred early in the crisis period and helped smooth policy changes. The Kim government continued to press forward with deregulation and liberalization, although not as rapidly or as comprehensively as some Koreans might have wished.

South Korea, however, remains characterized by vicious, polarizing political maneuvering that jeopardizes policy stability and saps the strength of elected presidents. With parliamentary elections scheduled for April 2000, political competition was heated throughout 1999. Ironically, despite the economic recovery, the Kim Dae Jung government's popularity and legitimacy eroded as allegations mounted of corruption, favoritism, and even suppression of the media. These allegations weakened the government's ability to push forward programs in a variety of areas, especially economic reform. Government efforts to force economic restructuring on the *chaebol*, for example, faltered. Some analysts believe that the South Korean recovery is more a matter of good fortune than economic policy reforms and corporate restructuring.

Favorable external factors include continued U.S. growth and the high value of the Japanese yen, which hobble Japanese competition. Nevertheless, increased consumption and imports suggest that Koreans generally feel more confident about their economic future.

Despite these internal difficulties, Kim Dae Jung's foreign policy initiatives, notably the Sunshine Policy toward North Korea, have thus far remained intact. However, a combination of a weakened position at home and further provocation by North Korea could undermine the political sustainability of this approach.

Part of the political challenge of the South Korean government is to show positive results for this Sunshine Policy. One consequence has been the separation of politics and business, allowing substantial economic cooperation and growing inter-Korean exchange. The Mt. Kumgang venture of the Hyundai business group has brought large numbers of tourists to the North Korean resort, and South Korean business interests are assisting in the construction of industrial parks in the North as well as the light water nuclear reactors being built under the U.S.–North Korean Agreed Framework. At the same time, South Korean humanitarian aid to the North is also increasing. Such activities may help build economic interdependence even in the absence of improved intergovernmental relations.

Critics of the Sunshine Policy, however, point out that these efforts have had no demonstrable effect on North Korean behavior. Problems in 1999 included a naval clash in June in addition to the detention of a South Korean tourist during the same month, allegedly for rudeness. North Korea has continued to rebuff the South's efforts to establish government-to-government dialogue on such practical issues of importance to South Koreans as family reunifications. Indeed, the Sunshine Policy illustrates the fundamental character of the Korean security dilemma. South Koreans regard the policy as a forward-looking approach to promote inter-Korean harmony, but the North Korean authorities view it as a scheme to bring down the regime through a subtle form of subversion.

Virtually no South Korean argues that the Sunshine Policy is so flawed that it should be abandoned. Rather, critics charge that the government has not been honest about the policy's reception in the North or realistic about its prospects. They contend that the South Korean government has oversold the policy, raising expectations of early, tangible results. Instead, the government should make it clear that while immediate benefits in terms of North Korean behavior may be unlikely, engagement remains the least harmful way of preventing armed conflict.

EXTERNAL SECURITY   The overall security environment in Northeast Asia is now less threatening than it has been for decades. South Korea enjoys good or improving relations with all its large power neighbors —China, Japan, and Russia—as well as a continuing strong alliance with the United States. However, the relations of these larger countries with each other are contentious, as exemplified by U.S. and Japanese concerns over China's longer-term political intentions, China's worries about U.S.-Japan-Taiwan relations and potential development of theater missile defense (TMD) systems, and China-Taiwan tensions over the status of Taiwan. The vulnerability of the atmosphere of Sino-American relations to incidents such as the U.S. bombing of the Chinese embassy in Belgrade and the allegations of Chinese theft of U.S. nuclear technology is troubling to South Korean analysts, who believe that good Sino-American relations are critical to regional security and particularly to efforts to contain possible North Korean adventurism.

The Korean Peninsula. Most South Koreans believe that a major war between the two Koreas is unlikely. North Korea, they believe, is not so irrational as to provoke a conflict that would endanger its very survival. Nonetheless, North Korea's constant military probing leads to incidents such as the June 1999 clash over fishing rights, when North Korea challenged the long-established "Northern Limit Line" border in the West Sea (Yellow Sea). This was the only major armed clash of 1999 and was of less strategic importance than North Korea's continuing efforts to develop weapons of mass destruction and missile delivery systems.

Two specific questions that preoccupied South Korea, Japan, and the United States during 1999 were the suspected underground nuclear site at Kumchang-ri, discovered in 1998, and North Korea's threat to launch another long-range Taepodong missile. Both these issues have been contained, for the moment, by negotiations between the United States and North Korea. Regarding Kumchang-ri, the United States agreed to provide food assistance to the North in exchange for inspection of the site. Inspection reassured the United States that the site could not presently be used for the development of nuclear weapons.

Negotiations surrounding the missile issue were more complicated. The United States, fearing the North's development of a long-range missile capable of striking Hawaii or Alaska, pressed for tight constraints on the full range of North Korean missile activities: exports, production, deployment, and flight testing. The short-term U.S. objective was to prevent Pyongyang from further testing of these missiles and to bar exports from North Korea of missiles and related equipment or technology. Bilateral talks in Berlin eventually resulted in an agreement whereby the United States would ease some economic sanctions against North Korea in return for a halt in further missile tests. The North also agreed to a continued freeze on its missile program as long as the United States continues active discussion on improving bilateral relations.

These agreements are consistent with the Kim Dae Jung government's policy of engagement as the only realistic and pragmatic option for dealing with North Korea. The report of former U.S. Defense Secretary William Perry, commissioned by the U.S. administration to review all aspects of U.S. policy toward North Korea and released on September 15, similarly emphasized the necessity of a two-path strategy of engagement plus continued military preparedness. Perry urged focus on weapons of mass destruction (WMD) and missiles as the most destabilizing aspects of North Korean policy.

The Berlin agreement and the Perry report help to increase stability in U.S.–North Korea relations, but progress is likely to remain slow. The WMD-missile issue will not easily be solved, as this is one of few bargaining chips North Korea has against the United States in support of its own survival. Thus, while the success of the negotiations provides grounds for some optimism that the North Korea conundrum can be managed, the denouement is not yet in sight and the basic situation remains volatile.

South Korea–U.S. Relations. Continuing insecurity on the Korean peninsula and the role of the United States in resolving problems underscore the importance of South Korea's alliance with the United States. The perspectives and assessments of Seoul and Washington have differed on some aspects of security policy, and domestic politics in both capitals are another complicating factor, making coordination of policy toward North Korea a constant challenge. Nevertheless, due in part to the Perry report, current U.S. policies now closely parallel those of the Kim government, and overall relations are generally sound.

However, the sensitivity of South Korea–U.S. relations was illustrated yet again in 1999 when allegations surfaced in the media of a massacre at No Gun Ri, early in the Korean War, of several hundred Korean civilians by American troops. These allegations led to protests and demands for compensation. The two governments were considering these issues as the year 2000 began.

DEFENSE POLICIES AND ISSUES

THE NORTH KOREAN THREAT   Most South Koreans believe that North Korea has not abandoned its strategy to communize the peninsula based on the principle of "One Chosun" (the name North Korea calls itself). According to the 1999 edition of the annual South Korean defense white paper, North Korea persists in its efforts, through propaganda and instigation, to foment social disorder in South Korea and to promote a united antigovernment front within South Korean society.

For its part, North Korea fears a German-style absorption by South Korea. It faces the dilemma that it must reform to survive, but that to open its society will lead to instability within its borders. The fear of undermining its own position prevents the leadership from pursuing significant market-oriented economic reforms, even as it accepts in principle the Chinese-Vietnamese formula of economic revitalization to bolster political legitimacy. The result has been a course of "muddling through." Despite all the discussion in South Korea and abroad in recent years about "soft" and "hard" North Korean landings, the current conventional wisdom in South Korea is that the North may continue to muddle through indefinitely.

In the meantime, the military threat from the North remains serious. The most worrisome scenario to South Koreans is the possibility that North Korea, feeling cornered, might lash out desperately. Although it seems improbable, and irrational, that Pyongyang would launch a suicidal attack in the face of a regime collapse, it cannot be completely discounted.

The North realizes that it cannot compete in conventional military terms, as demonstrated in 1999 by its humiliation in the West Sea (Yellow Sea) naval clash. Moreover, as a result of the Kosovo intervention, North Korea may have grown more fearful of attack by the United States. Therefore, despite serious food shortages and economic crises, the North has focused on developing modern weapons of mass destruction and associated missile delivery systems. Although the long-range Taepodong missile seems to make little direct difference to South Korea, which is already within range of Rodong missiles, it might shift the military balance of power in North Korea's favor.

Thus, the South Korean government believes that North Korea will cling tightly to the military card unless it can—and partly in order to—obtain a viable security guarantee from the United States. It is to break through this complex defensive psychology on the North's part that South Korea, together with the United States and Japan, is pursuing the strategy of comprehensive engagement with North Korea. The South Korean leadership believes that diplomacy is the best means to avoid the use of force.

DEFENSE BUDGET AND PROCUREMENT The 1997–1998 economic crisis led to restrictions on defense spending. The defense budget for 2000 is set at about 14.4 trillion won (US$12.7 billion at US$1 = 1,132 won), an increase of 5 percent from the 1999 level of approximately 13.7 trillion won (US$12.1 billion). Since 1985, the defense budget had increased by 9 to 10 percent every year, but in 1998 it dropped by 0.4 percent due to the financial crisis. The 1999 budget had been unsatisfactory to Ministry of National Defense officials, who had hoped for around 15.4 trillion won (US$13.6 billion). The defense budget represents 15.5 percent of the total state budget, and is concentrated on the development of sophisticated weaponry, on intelligence and surveillance and strike capability, and on research and development.

The draft budget allocates 37 percent to arms procurement. Major projects include domestic production of twenty KF-16 fighters between 2000 and 2005, procurement of a multiple launch rocket system (MLRS) and an army tactical missile system (ATACMS), and production of destroyers, submarines, and short-range air defense missiles. South Korea has also made an agreement with the United States to develop and manufacture missiles with a range of 300 kilometers (about 180 miles), and is looking for a way to develop and test longer-range missiles of 500 kilometers (about 310 miles) that could cover the entire Korean peninsula.

The South Korean government has reaffirmed that it has no plans to join the U.S.-initiated TMD program. In the government's view, TMD has many liabilities: high cost, overly sophisticated technology, and questionable effectiveness against North Korea's short-range missiles. Finally, pursuit of TMD would bring strong protests from China and Russia, both of which insist that it would trigger an arms race in Northeast Asia.

CONTRIBUTIONS TO REGIONAL SECURITY

KOREAN PENINSULA   The South Korean government has initiated policies of fostering a favorable security environment with the surrounding powers, particularly in the context of the Korean peninsula. It has strongly urged its U.S. and Japanese counterparts to engage North Korea rather than to confront or neglect it. For its part, the Kim Dae Jung administration has dropped its insistence that relations between North and South Korea be improved before the United States or Japan establishes diplomatic ties with North Korea.

South Korea–Japan cooperation is important to long-term stability in Asia and, more immediately, appears crucial to the success of the U.S.-initiated Agreed Framework and the Korean Peninsula Energy Development Organization's efforts to reduce nuclear weapons–related tension in Korea. South Korea increasingly recognizes the necessity of cooperation with Japan on issues concerning North Korea. The first-ever joint military exercise between the two countries took place in the East China Sea on August 5, 1999. Through the establishment of the Trilateral Coordination and Oversight Group (TCOG) in April 1999, consultation between the United States, South Korea, and Japan on issues concerning the Korean peninsula has also been improved. This is an important step as continuing differences in interests and priorities had led to mutual suspicion.

The South Korean government also coordinates closely with China, which it believes for the most part played a constructive role in the nuclear issue in 1994. In the missile issue in 1999, China might also have put pressure on North Korea in the hope that an incentive for TMD for the United States would be eliminated. North Korea is an economic burden on China, and China has encouraged North Korea to undertake economic reforms—in discussions with a visiting North Korean delegation headed by the chairman of North Korea's Supreme People's Assembly in September 1999.

South Korea, however, faces a dilemma in maintaining a strong security relationship with the United States and Japan while keeping relations with China amicable and cooperative. That is one reason why the South Korean government has ruled out any participation in the proposed TMD program for the time being, and why South Korea wants the United States and Japan to maintain friendly relations with China.

To South Korea, a truly effective arrangement on Korean peace also requires support from Russia. Visiting Russia in 1999 in large part to place South Korea–Russia relations, which had been strained following Russia's expulsion of a South Korean diplomat for spying in 1998, back on track, President Kim requested Russia's cooperation in his engagement policy toward North Korea. Russia has limited resources with which to help North Korea, even though Russia is currently attempting to mend fences with North Korea. During a February 2000 visit to North Korea by Foreign Minister Igor Ivanov, a new cooperation treaty, which emphasizes trade but excludes a military alliance, was signed.

Finally, South Korea has strengthened its bilateral relationship with Mongolia, another former ally of North Korea. The South Korean government has stated its position that Mongolia should be included in a multilateral security framework for the region.

MULTILATERAL   The South Korean government favors the initiation of so-called Six-Party Talks—to include China, Japan, Russia, and the United States—despite opposition to the idea at home and lack of interest from North Korea. The government believes that six-party or multilateral talks could deal with significant issues not covered in existing forums. It has also suggested that Southeast Asian nations and the three Northeast Asian nations—South Korea, China, and Japan—establish a new regional mechanism for economic and security cooperation for regional peace and development.

REGIONAL   Due to preoccupation with its own security and survival in a military standoff with North Korea, South Korea has very limited ability to contribute to wider regional security activities. Nevertheless, and despite strong public criticism, the government contributed combat troops to the International Force in East Timor (INTERFET) in September 1999. To the government, the contribution was acknowledgment that South Korea had itself been the beneficiary of such a force in 1950. It was also a demonstration of South Korea's willingness to stand up for democratic rights in other countries, a humanitarian gesture as a member of the international community, and an investment for future support in the event of crisis on the Korean peninsula. Participation in INTERFET may also have been a harbinger of a more active South Korean role in Asia Pacific security in the new millennium.

11 New Zealand

THE SECURITY ENVIRONMENT

New Zealand's strategic outlook is that of a small, affluent, self-absorbed, safe trading nation, geographically positioned flanking Australia and in the South Pacific but with links to Asia, North America, and Europe. As New Zealand heads to the new millennium, it is confronted by a unique set of security challenges.

New Zealand has possibly fewer direct challenges to its physical security than any other nation in the world. However, because New Zealand's economy is anchored by overseas trade, the stability of its external markets—split evenly between Australia, East Asia, North America, and Europe—and the security of its sea lines are critical. This interdependence means that New Zealand also has a stake in security challenges that confront its partners, and thus New Zealand's security is intertwined with that of the wider world. While the relatively small group of officials, politicians, journalists, and commentators who follow security affairs grasp this point, the public tends to take New Zealand's security for granted.

There is general political consensus that New Zealand should pursue a rules-based system for management of international relations. In practice, New Zealand's most important foreign relationships are managed bilaterally. The closing of the millennium was marked by a constructive approach to foreign affairs. The previous National Party–led government hosted the Asia-Pacific Economic Cooperation (APEC) gathering in Auckland in September 1999, which was the occasion for state visits by presidents Bill Clinton, Jiang Zemin, and Kim Dae Jung. The meeting facilitated the first official contact between China and the

United States since the mistaken U.S. bombing of the Chinese embassy in Belgrade, and afforded New Zealand opportunity to play a significant behind-the-scenes role in arranging the rapid international response concerning East Timor. New Zealand contributed over a thousand personnel to the INTERFET (International Force in East Timor) mission there—in addition to twenty-two personnel dispatched to peacekeeping operations around the world.

New Zealand's active role in regional affairs corresponds to an internal view that the country "punches above its weight," is an honest broker, and has a sensible voice in world affairs worth listening to. One measure of how other nations regard New Zealand was the election of former Labour Party Prime Minister Mike Moore as the first director-general of the World Trade Organization (for a three-year term, to be followed by Thailand's Supachai Panitchpakdi) and the election of former National Party Foreign Minister Don McKinnon as secretary general of the British Commonwealth.

Public opinion—and many politicians—take security for granted. However, the events of 1999 will deeply influence how specialists view the security of New Zealand in the new millennium. The sense that the end of the cold war ushered in a more peaceful world is now conditioned by clear evidence of the unpredictability of the region's economic and political stability. This nervousness is reinforced by continued tension in the Taiwan Strait and in the South China Sea, ballistic missile rivalry and possible theater missile defense systems in North Asia, and strategic competition in South Asia.

These negative trends were partially offset by positive developments. These included the speed with which regional leaders, especially China, agreed on a response to East Timor; China's willingness to show restraint in the latest cross-Strait incident, and the China-U.S. agreement on China's entry into the World Trade Organization (WTO) late in the year. On the economic side, evidence of recovery in Malaysia, South Korea, and Thailand bodes well for the future.

Of critical importance to New Zealand was the restoration of stable relations between China and the United States. Policymakers interpret this to have been achieved, at least for the time being, through the U.S. affirmation of the "one China" policy in response to Taiwan President Lee Teng-hui's provocative comments.

The situation in East Timor shook, for a short time, the widely held view that political instability would always be remote and irrelevant to New Zealand. The country witnessed how Indonesia, with a population of more than 210 million, could grow restive and unstable, a revelation that questioned assumptions about the nature of peace in the region as well. New Zealanders had believed that serious domestic insecurity would most likely occur in the South Pacific. East Timor showed that insecurity could occur right on the borders of Australia—which New Zealanders regard as being in their own immediate neighborhood. East Timor also demonstrated the complexity and danger of peacekeeping for New Zealand defense personnel.

One result of the East Timor crisis was reaffirmation of New Zealand's commitment to its defense relationship with Australia. At the political level, the relationship became closer than at any time since the sixties and seventies. New Zealand was the first country to support Australia in forming the intervention force, providing two C-130 transport aircraft, a frigate, and a naval tanker. The character of the relationship is likely to evolve further in the aftermath of the November election of a leftist Labour-Alliance minority government.

INFLUENCE OF THE DOMESTIC SITUATION   The East Timor crisis triggered a strong domestic reaction in New Zealand. Spurred by public opinion, the National Party government committed the largest military force to active service since Indonesia's "confrontation" with Malaysia in the mid-1960s. This decision was met with more than 80 percent public approval. Indeed, the government was widely criticized for not acting with greater urgency regarding East Timor—and even for not directly intervening.

Support for the military contribution in East Timor also briefly influenced broader public attitudes toward defense, widening the debate beyond the usual circles of politicians, specialists, and single-interest advocates. Social commentators, cartoonists, radio hosts, and a range of politicians strongly backed defense and criticized previous governments for not funding defense adequately. However, by the end of 1999 the debate had narrowed again.

The East Timor crisis overshadowed the debate over military armaments provoked by the Report of the Select Committee for Foreign Affairs, Defense and Trade into Defense Beyond 2000. The report had recommended that New Zealand downgrade its air-combat capability from twenty-two to ten F-16s and reduce the Navy from three to two surface combatants. The leftist Labour-Alliance minority government has committed itself to a review of the F-16 acquisition and to a two-frigate navy.

Recent events in the South Pacific attracted widespread public attention in New Zealand and reinforced the level of concern over stability in the South Pacific. The long-term security outlook for this subregion appears increasingly bleak. The Solomon Islands was plunged into conflict on the island of Guadalcanal, when militants drove thousands of Malaitans back to their home island as disputes over jobs and control of resources boiled over. In Samoa, which until recently has been remarkably peaceful, a reformist minister of public works was assassinated by political rivals. Bombings in Fiji's capital Suva remain unexplained.

Discussion in New Zealand concerning the security of the South Pacific tends to focus on ethnic conflict, urbanization, population growth, unemployment, land ownership, drugs, transnational crime, the sale of passports, people smuggling, illegal fishing, and natural disasters. There are differing opinions on the importance of the South Pacific to New Zealand. Some argue that the country's strong social linkages, and the fact of its geographical proximity, should make the South Pacific the primary focus of New Zealand's security policy. Others argue that, while New Zealand has unavoidable responsibilities in the South Pacific, Wellington should be mindful that its real interests lie in its trade and energy sources.

DEFENSE POLICIES AND ISSUES

RELATIONS WITH THE UNITED STATES   The former National Minister of Defense Max Bradford, accompanied by former Secretary of Defense Gerald Hensley, visited Washington in 1999, the first such visit since 1979. A subsequent meeting in Darwin with Australian Defense Minister John Moore, U.S. Defense Secretary Cohen, and Bradford encompassed issues relating to Indonesia and East Timor. This was the first formal discussion between Australian, U.S., and New Zealand ministers of defense since the 1984 ANZUS Council meeting that preceded the U.S.–New Zealand break over nuclear weapons policy. The increased tempo of U.S.–New Zealand high-level military-to-military visits continued. One was the visit of General Joseph Ralston, vice-chairman of the U.S. Joint Chiefs of Staff, to New Zealand in February 1999; another was the visit by the Chief of Defense Force, Air Marshall Carey Adamson, to the chairman of the U.S. Joint Chiefs of Staff, General Hugh Shelton, in June.

During his state visit to New Zealand in September, U.S. President

Clinton announced that the United States would consider exercises with New Zealand prior to the deployment of the East Timor mission. This represented a slight thaw in the ban placed by the United States on exercises with New Zealand forces following New Zealand's adoption of its nonnuclear stance, which still includes a ban on visits to New Zealand ports by nuclear-powered or nuclear-armed warships.

DEFENSE DOCTRINE   The ongoing development of defense doctrine noted in *Asia Pacific Security Outlook 1999* continues. New Zealand doctrine in general focuses on the development of interoperable force elements that can participate in joint and combined operations.

BUDGET   The size of New Zealand's defense budget is likely to be the subject of debate in 2000. There is general consensus that the budget should not be decreased, and some have even called for a substantial increase in defense funding. The new Labour-Alliance minority government, however, has ruled out any increase in defense spending. The cost of the East Timor commitment—up to NZ$75 million (US$39 million at NZ$1 = US$0.52)—will be the major defense issue for the immediate future.

MANPOWER AND PROCUREMENT   Here again, sustaining the force in East Timor represents the major issue facing the New Zealand Defense Force (NZDF). New Zealand's three-frigate naval combatant force is too limited to sustain two ships on station simultaneously.

CONTRIBUTIONS TO GLOBAL AND REGIONAL SECURITY

New Zealand's leading contribution to regional security was its hosting of the 1999 meetings of APEC, the region's only multilateral forum for heads of government. The former National Party government succeeded in injecting substance into the APEC trade liberalization process. Regional leaders committed themselves to a round of trade negotiations in the WTO, seeking elimination of export subsidies; the comprehensive liberalization of industrial products and services; the early liberalization of eight Accelerated Trade Liberalization Sectors, including fishing and forestry; placing competition and regulatory reform on the APEC Work Program; intensifying trade facilitation in areas such as customs procedures, and elimination of trade barriers; and developing a new set of banking standards for adoption by APEC economies.

Also during the APEC meetings, the then New Zealand minister of foreign affairs chaired a special meeting of APEC foreign ministers (plus Britain's Foreign Secretary Robin Cook) that formulated the basis of the international response to the East Timor crisis. Alongside the APEC gathering, New Zealand hosted the first bilateral meeting between Chinese President Jiang and U.S. President Clinton since the accidental U.S. bombing of the Chinese embassy in Belgrade.

The occurrence of the East Timor crisis just before the Auckland APEC meetings provided a test for New Zealand's quiet diplomacy. The National Party government resisted the temptation to play the East Timor issue for effect with the domestic audience, opting instead to work behind the scenes to encourage Asian leaders to attend the meeting once Indonesian President B. J. Habibie announced that he would not be present. The reward for this perseverance, despite criticism in the media, was the attendance at APEC of all other Asian leaders with the exception of Malaysia's Mahathir bin Mohamad.

At the ASEAN Regional Forum (ARF) in 1999, New Zealand was a full participant. The former National Party government viewed the ARF as an important mechanism for building confidence, broadly defined, in the region. However, the inability of the ARF or ASEAN to develop practical responses to the crises in the South China Sea or East Timor illustrated that neither multilateral institution is ready to take on active responsibility for conflict resolution.

The year 1999 saw the heaviest commitment of New Zealand defense forces to regional contingencies and global commitments in over thirty years. The government committed a frigate, a naval tanker, a battalion group, a field surgical team, four Iroquois helicopters, and two C-130 transport aircraft to the Australian-led, UN-sanctioned INTERFET operation in East Timor. In addition, New Zealand provided staff and liaison officers to this operation, including a one-star officer commanding the Dili area of operations. The New Zealand contribution peaked at over 1,200 personnel (over 10 percent of its defense force). Planning for this operation with Australia was a model of cooperation of combined forces, much improved over that seen during preparations for the Bougainville mission.

New Zealand forces dedicated to East Timor have worked very closely at the operational-tactical level with their counterparts from

Australia, Britain, Canada (whose infantry is integrated into a New Zealand battalion), and Ireland (which has a platoon of rangers under New Zealand battalion command as well).

The ANZAC-class frigate HMNZS *Te Kaha* served an eight-week tour with the Multinational Interception Force in the Persian Gulf late in 1999, after having been assigned as one of the warships to protect transport carrying INTERFET personnel and supplies to East Timor. Earlier, New Zealand had provided a six-person naval boarding team to U.S. Navy ships operating in the Gulf; the team returned to New Zealand in March.

All told, the former National Party government committed the country to twenty-three peacekeeping operations. Most significant has been INTERFET, but in addition, thirty-one defense personnel participated in the Australia-led operation in Bougainville; three staff are posted at UN headquarters to deal with issues related to the UN Special Commission (UNSCOM) in Iraq; officers are posted to the SFOR (Stabilization Force) Headquarters of the North Atlantic Treaty Organization in Bosnia as military observers; a rotating force of twenty personnel are integrated into British units in Bosnia; a New Zealand army officer is responsible for setting up a de-mining program in Kosovo, and de-mining assistance is being provided to Cambodia, Laos, and Mozambique; and small teams of specialists and observers have been deployed to the Sinai observation mission and to the UN Truce Supervision Organization (UNTSO) observer group in Jerusalem.

At the regional level, New Zealand participated in the biannual Five Power Defense Arrangements exercises along with Australia, Britain, Malaysia, and Singapore. New Zealand's contribution included a frigate, a naval tanker, and twelve A4K Skyhawk aircraft.

12 Papua New Guinea

THE SECURITY ENVIRONMENT

Papua New Guinea marks the twenty-fifth anniversary of its independence facing more serious internal than external threats. The most immediate and critical challenge, the twelve-year-long rebellion on the island of Bougainville, continues on a tortuous path toward a negotiated solution. A new potential problem is strengthened secessionist sentiment in the neighboring Indonesian province Irian Jaya.

INTERNAL   Papua New Guinea is a small, fragmented country, whose 4.7 million people speak more than seven hundred languages. In recent years, even its own political leaders have seen the country as politically unstable and lacking in administrative capability. All governments since independence have been coalitions, and no government has lasted a full term. Nevertheless, an essentially Westminster system has produced regular elections and smooth transitions, giving Papua New Guinea a continuous record of parliamentary democracy.

In July 1999, the scandal-ridden government of Prime Minister Bill Skate fell, after Skate resigned in a last-ditch gambit to win reelection through a parliamentary vote—rather than a national election—which he then lost. The new government of Sir Mekere Morauta, a respected former finance secretary and central bank governor, is viewed by many as more capable of bringing about fundamental improvements and reform than most recent governments have been.

Law and Order. Internal issues are the major security concern. Since the early 1970s, "tribal fighting" and the criminal activities of *raskol* gangs have plagued Papua New Guinea. In recent years, high-powered weapons—some allegedly obtained from the Papua New Guinea Defense Force (PNGDF)—have been used increasingly in tribal fighting and political feuds.

Under Prime Minister Skate, a self-confessed former *raskol*, there was a widespread perception that the central government itself was deeply penetrated by raskolism. Senior public offices became heavily politicized, and several senior ministers were mired in allegations of scandal. A special police investigation into "VIP crimes" was quashed, and the lead investigator subsequently sacked from the force.

The advent of the Morauta government brought signs of improvement. Large numbers of Skate appointees were dismissed. The officer in charge of the VIP investigation was reinstated as police commissioner, and the investigation was revived. In late 1999, Skate and his financial adviser, former World Bank official Pirouz Hamidian-Rad, were charged with fraud. Nevertheless, developing an honest and efficient government apparatus and restoring law and order remain major long-term challenges for the country.

The Bougainville Peace Process. A regional Peace Monitoring Group, led by an Australian military officer, remains in Bougainville to oversee the ceasefire that came into effect after an extended series of negotiations in April 1998 and assist in the process of reconciliation.

The PNGDF withdrew from Bougainville in August 1998, leaving only 150 personnel to assist the Royal Papua New Guinea Constabulary and Bougainvillean police reservists. But at the end of 1998, the peace process was jeopardized when PNG's parliamentary opposition, in protest against the Skate government, refused to extend special arrangements exempting Bougainville from the provincial and local-level government system established in 1995. The exemption had been a necessary condition in negotiations to establish the Bougainville Reconciliation Government, which combined rebel and government-backed elements. The crisis was overcome in January 1999 by an agreement to suspend the 1995-model government and to elect a new body to represent Bougainville in the negotiations.

In April 1999, talks held in New Zealand developed a preliminary framework for establishing a government on Bougainville, which would be in place until consideration of a package of political arrangements in June 1999. The framework included a body to plan and manage reconstruction as well as the disposal of weapons. However, leaders of the rebel Bougainville Revolutionary Army (BRA) rejected all terms of the framework except for the provision for creation of a new representative body. In May 1999, a Bougainville People's Congress (BPC) was duly elected, with former provincial premier Joseph Kabui named president. But by the end of 1999, only limited progress had been made toward finalizing governmental arrangements.

Shortly before losing office, Prime Minister Skate offered Kabui a "high level of autonomy" and a referendum on Bougainville's political future, while ruling out independence. In October, the new government under Morauta confirmed the offer of autonomy-but-no-independence and agreed to discuss a referendum.

As peace returns to Bougainville, divisions among Bougainvilleans have become more visible. Rebel leader Francis Ona and some other hard-liners refused even to participate in the negotiations. Other Bougainville leaders opposed the agreement to suspend the 1995-model government that had resolved the late 1998 impasse in negotiations; this group was led by former minister John Momis, who would have become governor under the 1995 system. However, Momis' position was strenuously resisted in central and south Bougainville, and in September the national parliament confirmed the suspension of the 1995 system. Other differences have arisen over such issues as the marketing of cash crops and the distribution of reconstruction funds.

In October 1999, Bougainville leaders set aside their differences and presented a common front in their negotiations with the national government. The resulting Nehan Resolution listed autonomy and a referendum as the primary demands. BPC President Kabui, however, made it clear that autonomy was not a final or sufficient solution, stipulating that there would be no arms disposal until the national government agreed to a referendum on independence. Minister for Bougainville Affairs Sir Michael Somare subsequently talked about the possibility of a constitutional amendment on autonomy in early 2000, but he argued that a referendum on independence was unconstitutional. A further meeting between Bougainville leaders and the national government in December produced the Hutjena Accord, which was designed to pave the way for "the highest possible autonomy for Bougainville." Somare also undertook to have the cabinet consider Bougainvillean demands for a referendum.

With the peace process already fragile, in November the PNG Supreme Court ruled that the suspension of the (never constituted) 1995-model of provincial government was illegal, thus undermining the legitimacy of the BPC. As 1999 ended, Bougainville leaders were seeking ways to prevent the peace process from unraveling. BRA claims of ceasefire violations by PNG security forces further threatened the peace.

EXTERNAL   In the words of the 1999 defense white paper, Papua New Guinea "is well placed to act as both a land and maritime bridge between Asia and the Pacific" and "to benefit from the ebb and flow of trade, investment and ideas between the two hemispheres of the New World." Its location has also given Papua New Guinea a relatively benign external security environment. However, developments in Indonesia since May 1998—and particularly the 1999 events in East Timor, which have reinforced separatist tendencies in the neighboring Indonesian province of Irian Jaya—have heightened recognition of the essential fragility of the present security situation. The 1996 defense white paper noted the country's vulnerability to intrusions into its air and maritime space, particularly by foreign fishing vessels, and to trafficking in arms and drugs. With the landing in Papua New Guinea of some sixty illegal "boat people" from China in 1999, these concerns were underscored.

Irian Jaya. In past years, activities of the Organisasi Papua Merdeka (OPM), or the Free Papua Movement, in neighboring Irian Jaya were the source of tension in relations with Indonesia, particularly when OPM freedom fighters sought refuge in Papua New Guinea. A 1986 treaty acknowledged these shared security concerns and set down arrangements for border management and liaison. In 1998, Papua New Guinea Prime Minister Skate and Indonesian President B. J. Habibie reconfirmed the commitment to cooperation and established a Joint Commission on Bilateral Cooperation. The commission will meet regularly to discuss issues including defense and security, trade and investment, and agriculture and human resource development. A border liaison meeting was held in September 1999.

While many in Papua New Guinea sympathize with the OPM, successive governments have supported Indonesian sovereignty in Irian Jaya. However, the movement toward independence by East Timor has strengthened both the Papuan independence movement and support for it within Papua New Guinea, raising the possibility of renewed tension along the border. In May 1999, the OPM was involved in a hostage-taking incident. Then PNGDF commander Major General Jerry Singirok had personally to negotiate the release of the hostages. With the withdrawal of most PNGDF personnel from Bougainville, the PNGDF has been able to resume limited patrol of its western border. In a departure from its earlier stance, it has offered to take part in coordinated patrols with the Indonesian military.

The Solomons. On its eastern border incursions by PNGDF troops into the Solomon Islands in pursuit of suspected BRA sympathizers were a cause of tension between the two countries during the Bougainville conflict. Cordial relations have since been restored, and the repatriation of Bougainvillean refugees in Honiara has commenced. However, changes of government and fiscal restraints have hampered border liaison and management and postponed an annual grant from Papua New Guinea to Solomon Islands. More significantly, the outbreak of fighting between the Solomon Islands government and the ethno-nationalist Guadalcanal Revolutionary Army has increased potential instability in this border area.

Australia. On Papua New Guinea's southern boundary with Australia, entry and exit of Australian border patrols have been facilitated by agreements reached in a meeting of the Papua New Guinea–Australia Torres Strait Advisory Council in Port Moresby in 1999.

Overall relations between Papua New Guinea and Australia, its former administering authority, have deteriorated in recent years. Generational change has weakened the personal ties that existed between the political leaders in the early independence period. Australian views of Papua New Guinea have been influenced by financial mismanagement and corruption, while Papua New Guinea officials see Australia as patronizing and as having failed to provide adequate support during the Bougainville crisis.

The election of Sir Mekere Morauta as prime minister resulted in marked improvement in relations between the two countries. Australia promised increased development assistance and offered to assist in renewed negotiations with the World Bank and the International Monetary Fund. At the Asia-Pacific Economic Cooperation (APEC) meetings in New Zealand in September 1999, a "Friends of Papua New Guinea" group, led by Australia, New Zealand, and China, promised further assistance. Subsequently, the larger World Bank–led Consultative Group of Papua New Guinea aid donors agreed to a package of around US$300 million to support structural reform.

China/Taiwan. In part reflecting the progressive weakening of the "special relationship" with Australia in the 1980s, Papua New Guinea adopted a "Look North" foreign policy emphasizing relations with Asia. In December 1998, Prime Minister Skate visited China to discuss closer ties, returning with a promise of budgetary assistance. Thus, it came as a surprise when, in July 1999, it was reported that Skate (who was facing a parliamentary no-confidence vote) had visited Taiwan, secured promises of US$2.3 billion in budgetary assistance and loans, and signed a communiqué establishing formal diplomatic ties.

The Chinese government reacted angrily, lodging a strong protest over "a serious infringement upon China's sovereignty" and threatening unspecified "serious consequences." However, when Morauta took office later in July, the government reverted to the previous one-China policy, noting that Skate had not followed normal procedures in recognizing Taiwan. Further fence mending was done in a visit to Beijing by the foreign minister and at a meeting between Morauta and Chinese President Jiang Zemin during the APEC forum, both in October. China subsequently agreed to provide US$10 million in budgetary assistance and aid projects.

The Morauta government has also pledged to maintain cooperation with Taiwan, which has long had a representative in Papua New Guinea, and which Papua New Guinea has recognized in the areas of economy, trade, technology, and international cooperation since 1995.

DEFENSE POLICIES AND ISSUES

Although the primary constitutional function of the PNGDF is to defend the country, the military has had relatively little to do in external security. Rather, it has been increasingly involved in maintaining domestic law and order. This became particularly prominent after the Bougainville conflict broke out in 1988 and in 1991 was formally designated the highest priority. However, the PNGDF has been handicapped in performing its mission by persistent problems with funding, equipment, training, and discipline.

In external security, the major activities of the PNGDF have been to patrol the country's western and—especially during the Bougainville conflict—eastern borders, and to police the waters of its 200-mile economic zone, primarily for illegal fishing. The maritime responsibilities and accompanying requirements of the PNGDF were spelled out in 1999 with the publication of *Fundamentals of Maritime Doctrine*. A major initiative is the planned acquisition of a powerful new surveillance satellite earth station network, with stations in the provinces of West Sepik, Central, and New Ireland. This will boost Papua New Guinea's capacity to control illegal fishing, drug trafficking, arms dealing, and people smuggling in its waters. The network is to be constructed for the National Fisheries Authority and the Defense Force National Surveillance Organization.

White Paper. With progress made toward peace on Bougainville, the government has taken the opportunity to review the priorities of the PNGDF. The review resulted in the publication in 1999 of a new defense white paper, replacing that of 1996. Although it makes no radical departure from previous policy, the 1999 paper argues that the PNGDF should de-emphasize its internal security role and focus on its three other constitutional functions: defending sovereignty and national interests, contributing to regional and collective security, and nation building and development. Underlining this "new" emphasis, the white paper is entitled "Service to Others." Implementing the commitment to nation building and development, the defense force has begun work on a Regional Engineering Base in Western Highlands and plans to establish two more such bases in Madang and Kimbe in West New Britain.

The practical impact of the new PNGDF emphasis remains to be seen. The white paper calls for a "judicious rebuilding of PNGDF capabilities to meet sovereignty requirements," but notes that if this is achieved and if engineer and medical capabilities are strengthened, no special measures will be required for the other roles. Priority areas are identified as improved maritime capacity (the proposed acquisition of two additional patrol boats and an operations support ship); strengthening of air capability (fixed- and rotary-wing aircraft to provide air transport, medical evacuation, search and rescue, surveillance, and minimum capability for close air support for ground troops and maritime interdiction); and the creation of a third army battalion.

Forces and Funding. The new white paper endorses the 1996 white paper's recommendations for a "smaller, more mobile and capable force," and for improved intelligence. It also proposes the reactivation of the PNG Volunteer Rifles as a reserve force to assist in law and order and internal security operations, and reintroduction of a school cadet scheme. Following another recommendation, the PNGDF in 1999 recruited women as soldiers for the first time.

The 1999 white paper envisages a reduction in PNGDF size by about 18 percent to 4,309 personnel, with an additional reserve force of 112. At the end of 1999, however, force size stood at 4,500, a reduction of only 100 from the previous year. Defense expenditures for the year 2000 are K85 million (US$27.87 million at US$1 = K3.05), K5 million

(US$1.64 million) above the budgeted 1999 figure; this represents 2.8 percent of total government spending and 0.9 percent of gross national product.

While both the Skate and Morauta governments have supported strengthening the capability of the PNGDF and addressing discipline and morale issues, problems remain. On coming to office in July 1999, the Morauta government suspended General Singirok, who now faces a reactivated charge of sedition dating from a 1997 incident during his previous term as military commander. In his place, one of several senior officers Singirok had retired in 1998 was appointed as acting commander. However, this move did not resolve the problems of politicization and of factionalism, which was largely regional. In September, PNGDF troops threatened to withdraw from Bougainville, in protest against poor food (mainly resulting from nonpayment to local suppliers) and nonpayment of salaries and allowances. Although the immediate situation was resolved, it highlights continuing problems of provisioning PNGDF personnel, notwithstanding the promised increase in the defense budget.

International Cooperation and Assistance. Australia continues to be the major foreign partner and source of assistance for the PNGDF. In the aftermath of the abortive 1997 "Sandline" affair, in which the central government contracted foreign mercenaries to put down the Bougainville rebellion, the Papua New Guinea and Australian defense ministers signed a joint statement entitled "The New Defense Partnership." The partnership identified several key principles—mutuality, openness and transparency, respect, regular dialogue, achievability, and democracy—and sought to focus on a set of core activities—internal security and external defense, regional security, training and education, and other activities, including joint exercises.

During 1999, the PNGDF participated in two joint naval exercises, both involving Australia. These were "Paradise 99," sponsored by Papua New Guinea, in which PNGDF patrol boats, landing craft, and a barge participated with Australian and, for the first time, Indonesian naval vessels, and the Australian-sponsored Kakadu exercise, involving naval contingents from New Zealand and ASEAN countries.

Despite close cooperation with Australia, Papua New Guinea defense officials and senior PNGDF officers seek diversified military ties and reduced dependence on Australian assistance. This is consistent with the universalist principles of Papua New Guinea's foreign policy, reinforced by the "Look North" emphasis. The PNGDF also has agreements on the status of forces or memoranda of understanding with Indonesia, Malaysia, New Zealand, the United States, and Israel. The U.S. Coast Guard is assisting in the training of personnel for the new maritime surveillance system.

CONTRIBUTIONS TO REGIONAL AND GLOBAL SECURITY

Internationally, Papua New Guinea is a minor actor, limited by size and financial resources. However, it does take part in regional and international forums. It has been particularly outspoken in opposing nuclear testing, supporting human rights in and beyond the region, and expressing concerns on environmental issues.

Papua New Guinea is a member of the Pacific Islands Forum (formerly the South Pacific Forum), with a seat on its Regional Security Committee, and is a leading force in the Melanesian Spearhead Group. Its previous defense white paper supported formation of a regional peacekeeping force and recommended the establishment of defense relations with Tonga, Fiji, and members of the Melanesian Spearhead Group as a first step. The 1999 white paper includes no specific reference to the regional peacekeeping force, but reiterates the government's commitment to regional surveillance and "selected peacekeeping, peace enforcement and other collective security and coalition operations."

In Southeast Asia, Papua New Guinea maintains its "Special Observer" status in the Association of Southeast Asian Nations (ASEAN). It participates in the wider ASEAN Regional Forum and APEC.

After the East Timor referendum in August 1999, the Papua New Guinea government welcomed the vote for independence and expressed its "desire to give assistance during the transitional period." Subsequently Defense Minister Alfred Pogo, responding to requests from Australia, announced that Papua New Guinea would send troops to East Timor if requested by the Indonesian government. However, the government later said that, due to resource constraints, Papua New Guinea could not participate in the international force, although it might join a later phase of the peacekeeping operation.

13 Philippines

THE SECURITY ENVIRONMENT

The Philippines faces difficult challenges in the year 2000. The economy has shown signs of improving, but it has not yet fully recovered from the Asian financial crisis. The administration of President Joseph Estrada has been beset by political controversies, and the government has had to confront the intensified activities of communist insurgents and Muslim secessionists. Externally, the situation in the South China Sea appears to be worsening, as China and other country claimants build and improve structures on disputed reefs.

DOMESTIC POLITICS Since Joseph Estrada assumed the presidency of the Philippines in the middle of 1998, his administration has seemingly been mired in one controversy after another. There has been division over the government's handling of the assets left behind by Ferdinand Marcos, accusations of government interference with the press, and resistance to proposals for amending the constitution.

Talk in 1999 of a compromise with the Marcos family to resolve the assets left by the former president badly split public opinion. The government's subsequent use of the Marcos escrow account as collateral for foreign loans, in tandem with reports of a US$13 billion Swiss bank account in the name of Marcos's daughter Irene Marcos-Araneta, further complicated matters.

In mid-1999, the administration was accused of curtailing freedom of the press, after the *Manila Times*, a major daily that had been critical of Estrada, was taken over by an ally of the president and then closed down. Estrada was also accused of pressuring advertisers to withdraw support from another newspaper critical of his administration.

Moves to amend the 1987 constitution proved divisive. The government proposed to amend provisions regarding foreign investment by, for example, allowing businesses to have 100 percent foreign ownership. Opponents of the government proposals fear that this process could threaten key political provisions of the constitution, such as term limits. Public opposition to these proposals, in addition to public concern over the perceived cronyism and threats to press freedom, resulted in large rallies in August and September. These rallies were supported by such prominent figures as former President Corazon Aquino and Cardinal Jaime Sin.

These issues contributed to the continuing plunge in Estrada's net approval rating, from 65 percent in June 1999, to 28 percent in October, to 5 percent at the end of the year. There is widespread expectation of a cabinet change in 2000.

THE ECONOMY   The Philippines appears to be recovering from the Asian financial crisis. Its gross domestic product, which contracted by 0.5 percent in 1998, grew by 1.2 percent in the first quarter of 1999 and was estimated to grow by 2.6–3.2 percent for the year. (Gross national product, which grew by only 0.1 percent in 1998, expanded by 3 percent in the first three quarters of 1999 and was projected to grow by 3.5–4 percent for the whole of 1999.) Government statistics indicate that inflation stayed in single digits in 1998 and 1999 (at 6.6 percent for the first three quarters of 1999), a record the government hopes to sustain in 2000. However, economic analysts fear that oil price and wage hikes will increase inflation.

Other positive indicators include declining unemployment, increasing agricultural production and yields (the target of major government programs), and a current account surplus for 1998. The peso stabilized at P37–39 to the U.S. dollar in the first quarter of 1999, but then fluctuated to above P40 in the third and fourth quarters. Renewed volatility of the peso underlined the country's still incomplete economic recovery, contrary to the president's claims in his State of the Nation Address in July 1999.

INTERNAL SECURITY   Internal security concerns are dominated by local communist and Muslim insurgent movements. Organized crime also receives priority government attention. Once thought to be waning, the communist and Muslim rebels are regaining strength, partly as a consequence of the economic crisis. The secretary of national defense projected the strength of the communist New People's Army (NPA) at 9,463 in June 1999, up 5 percent from 1998. NPA's stock of arms is believed to have grown fivefold during the same period. Peace negotiations with the NPA were suspended in February 1999 after the rebels abducted an army general and several officers. Talks with the communist political arm, the National Democratic Front (NDF), broke off in May after the Netherlands-based NDF leadership protested the Philippines' ratification of the Philippines-U.S. Visiting Forces Agreement (VFA). Nevertheless, the government is pursuing peace talks with the local communists, even without the involvement of their leaders.

Similarly, in Mindanao, the Moro Islamic Liberation Front (MILF), now the largest secessionist group, expanded to an estimated 15,415 personnel in June 1999, up by nearly two thousand from 1998, its largest membership since 1986. Former fighters from the Moro National Liberation Front (MNLF), which concluded a peace agreement with the government in 1996, may have joined the MILF.

The government has also been trying to launch peace negotiations with the MILF, but this effort foundered in 1999 over MILF insistence that the government officially recognize its camps and refrain from entering them; clashes between MILF and government forces continued. A new round of talks scheduled for December was canceled by the MILF, apparently because the Philippine government refused to allow the MILF to meet with new Indonesian President Abdurrahman Wahid during his visit to Manila in late November. Furthermore, according to a ranking MILF leader, East Timor's achievement of independence has inspired the group to continue its struggle for a separate Islamic state in Mindanao.

The smallest rebel force, the Abu Sayaf Group, with an estimated 1,157 soldiers, also continues to conduct criminal and terrorist activities in the southern Philippines. However, these activities are not on the scale of previous years.

Meanwhile, for the third time, an election for officials of the Autonomous Region in Muslim Mindanao (ARMM) has been postponed, from September 1999 to September 2000. This was apparently done to include the residents of any additional provinces that opt to join the ARMM in an upcoming plebiscite, but it further delays formalizing the autonomy arrangement for this region agreed to in 1996.

The Estrada administration continues to emphasize its fight against organized crime. Recognizing the links between domestic and international criminal groups, Estrada created the Philippine Center on Transnational Crime (PCTNC) in January 1999. PCTNC will supervise the anticrime operations of all government agencies, establish a central database and conduct research, and coordinate information exchanges with other agencies, foreign governments, and international organizations.

FOREIGN POLICY AND EXTERNAL SECURITY The Philippines' foreign policy remains anchored by three principles: preservation of territorial integrity and national security, largely through diplomacy and cooperation with other states; promotion of development through economic diplomacy; and the protection of the rights and welfare of the large number of overseas Filipinos.

South China Sea. The external environment of the Philippines is relatively peaceful except for problems arising out of disputes over territorial and boundary claims in the South China Sea. While the press speculated that the government exaggerated this issue in 1999 in order to gain Senate approval of the VFA, there are legitimate causes for concern. Given the limitations of the Philippines' military capabilities, policymakers believe that raising the issue in international forums is the best way to restrain other claimants from actions that could undermine Philippine interests in the area.

After China renovated its structures on Mischief Reef in 1998, bilateral Expert Group Meetings on confidence-building measures were held in Manila in March and in Beijing in October, but with no conclusive results. The Philippines proposed a regional code of conduct in the South China Sea and called on China to dismantle its structures on the reef; China rejected the proposals. Although China had earlier offered joint use of the structures, in these meetings China argued that the time for joint use would be "ripe" only when (1) the improvements are finished and an administrative and management system is in place, (2) Philippines-China relations are normalized, and (3) fishing arrangements and cooperation are established. Joint use now appears unlikely. A planned visit to China in May 1999 by President Estrada was canceled due to China's persistent activities on Mischief Reef.

In the meantime, the Philippines has stepped up naval surveillance and patrol in the area, and there have been several incidents. In May, a Chinese fishing vessel sank near the contested Scarborough Shoal after colliding with a Philippine Navy ship in rough waters as Philippine personnel were preparing to board the vessel. China demanded US$30,000 in compensation; the Philippine government refused, arguing that the sinking was accidental and took place in Philippine waters. In July, another sinking of a Chinese fishing vessel occurred, this time near the Philippine-occupied Likas (West York) Island and Panata (Lankiam) Cay. A Philippine Navy ship approaching Thitu Island encountered two Chinese vessels, fired warning shots, and gave chase. One Chinese boat collided with the ship and sank. Manila said this was also an accident, but expressed regret; Beijing called it a "serious incident."

In November, China threatened to remove forcibly a Philippine Navy ship that ran aground on Scarborough Shoal, contending that this was a Philippine tactic to occupy the shoal; Manila insisted this was an accident. The Philippines tried to remove the ship before Chinese Prime Minister Zhu Rongji's visit to Manila for the ASEAN (Association of Southeast Asian Nations) Informal Summit in late November, but was unable to do so until after the meetings.

At the same time, other claimant countries have begun to strengthen their physical presence and build structures on contested areas in the South China Sea. In June, Malaysia occupied Pawikan (Investigator) Shoal; in August, it built on Gabriela Silang (Erika) Reef; and in October, Vietnam improved its structures on Barque (Canada) Reef, Osmena (Cornwallis) Reef, and De Jesus (Allison) Reef. Also in October, Vietnamese troops on Tennent Reef fired on a Philippine Air Force reconnaissance plane conducting an aerial survey of the expansion of structures on the reef. These actions by fellow ASEAN members prompted the Philippines to file diplomatic protests.

Incidents such as these have raised concern among Philippine defense officials regarding the stability of the South China Sea. The secretary of national defense has proposed that the Philippines also improve its structures in areas it occupies and construct new ones on other Philippine-claimed-but-not-yet-occupied reefs or shoals. Defense officials believe the South China Sea dispute is becoming a serious problem requiring greater defense effort.

Relations with the United States. After long debate, the Philippine Senate ratified the VFA on May 27, 1999. The VFA makes possible the resumption of large-scale bilateral military exercises in the Philippines. These include the Balikatan Exercise, the largest joint and combined exercise series between the two countries, which was suspended in 1997 due to the absence of a legal framework governing the status of U.S. forces while in Philippine territory.

Ratification of the VFA has completed the reconstruction of Philippines-U.S. defense relations after the end of the Military Bases Agreement in 1991. In October, the two governments announced that experts would meet to discuss the needs of the Armed Forces of the Philippines (AFP) for both defense and humanitarian missions. President Estrada claims that U.S. President Bill Clinton, during the September Asia-Pacific Economic Cooperation (APEC) summit in New Zealand, reassured him that the United States would defend the Philippines against foreign aggression.

DEFENSE POLICIES AND ISSUES

PRIORITIES   The Department of National Defense has set six key defense priorities for the country:
- Resolution of the internal security problems;
- Contribution to regional peace and stability;
- Rebuilding the AFP into a modern and professional force;
- Increased participation in nation building;
- Effective response to crisis situations; and
- Efficient defense resource management.

Based on these priorities, the Defense Department has developed a Five-Point Strategy of "Defend-Respond-Build-Promote-Prepare" for national defense. Significant aspects of this strategy are as follows:
- Defense, based on the principle of self-reliance.
- Response to crises, including natural disasters, such as typhoons, earthquakes, and volcanic eruptions.
- Nation building, including support for law enforcement agencies in fighting criminal activities such as arms smuggling, drug trafficking, illegal migration, money laundering, piracy, and terrorism.
- Promotion of regional and global security, requiring good relations with countries in the region, especially through multilateral mechanisms.
- Preparation, involving the modernization of equipment and doctrine, and the professionalization of AFP personnel.

MODERNIZATION   In 1995, the Philippine Congress authorized the modernization of the AFP. The program developed by the AFP aims to provide a "basic minimum defense capability" within fifteen years. It has five main components: (1) force restructuring and organizational development; (2) capability, matériel, and technology development; (3) bases and support systems development; (4) human resource development; and (5) doctrine development.

DEFENSE BUDGET   The Philippines has one of the lowest defense budgets, relative to national budget and GNP, in the region. The defense budget covers the AFP as well as civilian agencies under the Department of National Defense.

The total defense budget for 1999 was P51.574 billion (US$1.28 billion at US$1 = P40.3), which constituted only 8.7 percent of the national budget (of P588.098 billion, or US$14.59 billion) and approximately 1.7 percent of projected GNP. The AFP budget was P39.62 billion (US$983.12 million), 6.7 percent of the national budget and approximately 1.3 percent of projected GNP.

Of the 1999 AFP budget, 79 percent went to personnel services, 20 percent to maintenance of weapons and equipment, and 1 percent to capital outlay (down from 4 percent the previous year). By component, the army received 31 percent of the 1999 budget, the air force 14 percent, the navy 15 percent, and general headquarters 11 percent.

PROCUREMENT   Due to the financial crisis, in 1998 President Estrada suspended acquisition of new weapons and equipment for the AFP. However, in April 1999 he authorized the resumption of military acquisitions. Priorities for the next five years include the multirole fighter (MRF) to improve air defense; offshore patrol vessels (OPV) to patrol the Exclusive Economic Zone (EEZ); air defense radar; long-range patrol aircraft; command and control systems; and firepower, mobility, communications, and intelligence capability for the army and marines. The MRF and OPV projects are now in the bidding process. The president also approved the allotment of P6 billion (US$149 million) for acquisition of equipment and weapons.

INTERNAL SECURITY OPERATIONS   The basic responsibility for suppressing internal security threats was delegated to the Philippine National Police (PNP) in 1995, but the PNP Reform and Reorganization Act of 1998 transferred internal security operations (ISO) back to the AFP. The president would like to end the insurgency problem within three years. Thus, the AFP is now reorienting its modernization program, which had been directed primarily toward external defense, to respond to the new ISO-related obligations.

Contributions to Regional and Global Security

REGIONAL   The Philippines continues to put a premium on participation in regional institutions. It hosted the 3rd ASEAN Informal Summit in late November 1999, which was attended as well by the heads of government of China, Japan, and South Korea. Agreements reached at the summit included elimination of import duties by 2010 for long-standing members and by 2015 for the new members, the establishment of a troika of the current, past, and future heads of the ASEAN Standing Committee to consult between summits, and increased coordination with China, Japan, and South Korea.

The Philippines drafted and presented to the summit a proposed regional Code of Conduct to govern actions by claimants in the South China Sea, but the summit failed to convince China to endorse the code. Nevertheless, the Philippines continues to adhere to the Manila Declaration on the South China Sea, and to exercise self-restraint with regard to disputes. It encourages other claimants to do the same and to settle disputes peacefully. While other claimants have renovated existing structures and occupied new reefs and shoals, the Philippines has not followed their lead. Furthermore, it has undertaken bilateral confidence-building measures particularly with China, while still encouraging multilateral approaches to the problem.

The Philippines also remains an active participant to the ASEAN Regional Forum (ARF) and the APEC process. It attended the ARF Inter-sessional Support Group (ISG) on confidence-building measures meetings in March and October, and participated in the annual ARF ministerial meeting in July. It took part in the Auckland APEC meetings in September. In addition, it participates in unofficial mechanisms such as the Council for Security Cooperation in Asia Pacific (CSCAP) and the Pacific Economic Cooperation Council (PECC).

During the 32nd ASEAN Ministerial Meeting in Singapore in July 1999, the Philippines exhorted fellow ASEAN members to move forward in "strengthening the foundation and building the superstructure of peace and security in ASEAN and the wider region of East Asia." It emphasized that, while existing mechanisms such as the ARF, bilateral defense cooperation and joint border patrols, and multilateral confidence-building measures have had positive impacts, there is need still to move toward establishing mechanisms for preventive diplomacy and conflict resolution.

The Philippines recognizes the importance of peacekeeping operations. In September 1999, it contributed 247 soldiers to the United Nations–sanctioned International Force in East Timor (INTERFET) and was prepared to send as many as 1,000 personnel. In addition, the Philippine Committee on Humanitarian Mission arrived in East Timor in October.

Bilateral Relations. High-level visits are a principal mechanism for enhancing the Philippines' bilateral relationships. In 1999, visits to other ASEAN members included the president's state visit to Brunei in August, and visits by the AFP chief of staff to Indonesia, Singapore, and Thailand in October. The president also traveled to Japan and South Korea in June and to Argentina and Chile after the APEC meetings in September. The Philippines hosted Venezuelan President Hugo Chavez in October and new Indonesian President Wahid in November.

The Philippines continues to cultivate its bilateral alliance with the United States. The government contends that the VFA contributes to regional security by providing another mechanism through which the United States can maintain its commitment and visibility in the region, something regional states consider important to peace and stability. With ratification of the VFA, the alliance appears to have renewed dynamism; however, it remains to be seen whether it will be a functioning instrument for promoting their common and national strategic interests.

The Philippines has memoranda of understanding or agreements on defense cooperation with numerous countries, including Australia, France, Indonesia, Malaysia, Singapore, South Korea, Spain, Thailand, and the United Kingdom. In April 1999, the Philippines and Spain signed a bilateral Treaty of Friendship and Cooperation, which consolidates mutual cooperation on political, economic, and social development.

GLOBAL   The Philippines' main contribution to global security is its participation in UN activities for the prevention and management of conflict, disarmament, and arms control. The Philippines was elected vice-chairman of the 1999 Substantive Session of the United Nations Disarmament Commission (UNDC) in April, and called for "practical disarmament of conventional and other weapons." It advocated convening the Fourth Special Session of the UN General Assembly Devoted to Disarmament (SSOD IV). The Philippines also participates in UN relief operations, and it recently offered to host a peacekeeping operations workshop.

14 Russia

The Security Environment

As Russia enters the twenty-first century, its leaders perceive a bleak security environment. They see a growing internal security threat in the North Caucasus and a loss of international influence as the United States and the North Atlantic Treaty Organization (NATO) choose to ignore Russia and threaten its interests. A new security concept developed in 1999 reflects these changed perceptions and a corresponding reassertion of Russian national pride and standing.

INTERNAL   For Russia, the year 2000 marks a decade of post-Communist democratic development and economic marketization. Though severe challenges and uncertainties remain, achievements, albeit modest in absolute terms, are impressive in light of previous history.

Russia experienced constant political turbulence in 1999. There were two replacements of the prime minister, a failed attempt to impeach the president, financial and corruption scandals involving the first family and top politicians, a vicious parliamentary election campaign, and the surprise resignation of President Boris Yeltsin and transfer of power to Prime Minister Vladimir Putin on the last day of the year. Nevertheless, Russians elected a new parliament in December 1999 and will hold a presidential election in 2000. Despite the drama, the country appears to be moving toward the political center.

Internal security has been severely challenged by new conflict in the North Caucasus and terrorism in Moscow and elsewhere in the country. In early August, federal forces in the Dagestan Republic were surprised by a cross-border incursion from Chechnya. It took the army several weeks to repel the invasion. In August and September, five powerful explosions in residential areas of Moscow and two southern Russian towns claimed some three hundred lives. The government and public opinion blamed the Chechens, and newly appointed Prime Minister Putin declared war on terrorism. In late September, the military launched an offensive in Chechnya. The second Chechen war was prosecuted more effectively than the first, but there were still hundreds of casualties on both sides, over two hundred thousand refugees, and widespread damage. It also became a sticking point in Russia's relations with the United States and Europe.

Relations between Moscow and other regions, including the Russian Far East, remain generally calm. Even the controversial governor of the Maritime province patched up relations with the Kremlin in 1999. Except in the North Caucasus, there is no danger of political separatism.

Russia is slowly recovering from the 1998 financial crisis. A sharp devaluation of the ruble boosted industrial production by 9 percent in 1999, gross domestic product increased 0.9 percent, and the trade balance benefited from a doubling of world oil prices. Inflation, however, remained high at 120 percent. Despite difficulties with the International Monetary Fund (IMF) and international creditors, economic prospects beyond 2000 are mildly encouraging. It will take a long time, however, before recovery reaches Siberia and the Russian Far East.

EXTERNAL   Russia's leaders see the country's broadest security interest as preserving or restoring its status as a major power. Conversely, the principal threats are attempts to ignore Russia or to keep it from having the influence of a major power. Shaken by U.S. willingness to disregard Russian views on such issues as Kosovo and Iraq, the leadership now takes a more pessimistic view of the conflicting trends toward unipolarity and multipolarity in the post–cold war era. It believes that U.S. power is expanding unchecked and that a multipolar world remains a distant prospect. To right the balance, Moscow looks to countervailing alliances with countries independent of the United States—countries such as China, India, and Iran.

NATO again is seen as Moscow's main security problem. Actions offensive to Russia include the formal admission to NATO of three Eastern European members in early 1999, NATO's intervention in Yugoslavia without a UN Security Council mandate in March, and the announcement of NATO's new strategic concept emphasizing out-of-area activities in April. When the Kosovo campaign began, Moscow froze all contacts with the alliance—but without formally suspending the 1997 Russia-NATO Founding Act. In June, Russian troops joined NATO forces in the Kosovo Force (KFOR), and two months later Russia's military representative returned to Brussels; but Russia's cooperation with NATO remains limited to Kosovo and Bosnia.

These developments have caused serious deterioration in relations with the United States. Symbolically, in March 1999, en route to the United States, Prime Minister Yevgeny Primakov ordered his plane to turn back when he learned of imminent NATO strikes against Yugoslavia. Relations were superficially patched up in a brief meeting between Yeltsin and U.S. President Bill Clinton at the Group of Eight summit in Cologne in June, but soon soured due to the money laundering scandal and then Chechnya. U.S. Defense Secretary William Cohen's trip to Russia in September achieved modest success in resuming cooperation in areas such as missile early warning and the Y2K problem.

Russia's ties with the European Union are also strained due to the Chechnya war, after improvement earlier in 1999 when Russian and EU representatives jointly persuaded Yugoslavian President Slobodan Milosevic to withdraw from Kosovo and accept an international force. Moscow reacted favorably to the European Union's "Common Strategy on Russia," enunciated in June. However, the EU-Russia summit in Helsinki in October featured stormy European criticism of Russia over Chechnya.

The Former Soviet Union. Relations with Commonwealth of Independent States (CIS) members have further varied. Integration with Belarus was pushed largely by Minsk, proceeded to a signed treaty, but fell far short of a merger. The other major CIS states, Ukraine and Kazakhstan, consolidated their political independence.

A major blow to Moscow was the refusal of Uzbekistan, Georgia, and Azerbaijan, in spring 1999, to continue participation in the 1992 Tashkent Collective Security Treaty (CST). The remaining CST members—Armenia, Belarus, Kazakhstan, the Kyrgyz Republic, Russia, and Tajikistan—are cooperating more closely, especially in air defense. But the three "refuseniks," plus Ukraine and Moldova (which never joined the CST), have formed a loose association named GUUAM (after the countries' initials), with political support from the United States. GUUAM is widely viewed in Moscow as anti-Russian.

In Central Asia in 1999, Russia phased out its military presence. In Kazakhstan, it had to reduce the leasing of test ranges and pay back rent for the Baikonur space center. In Kyrgyz, it bowed to local pressure to withdraw its border troops. Turkmenistan asked for the removal of Russia's remaining military presence.

However, some Central Asian regimes are again turning to Moscow for help. Russian arms and advisers will be sent to Kyrgyz, whose government was challenged in August 1999 by Islamic rebels. In Tajikistan, Russia's regional stronghold in Central Asia, Moscow remained committed to maintaining a substantial military presence. Uzbekistan, despite its withdrawal from the Tashkent pact, is interested in maintaining contacts with Russia. Turkmenistan has expressed interest in technical assistance.

Asia Pacific. Since Kosovo, Moscow has emphasized building a loose coalition with China and India as a counterweight to perceived U.S. hegemony. This was the message at the August 1999 Bishkek summit of the "Shanghai Five"—China, Kazakhstan, Kyrgyz, Russia, and Tajikistan. The declaration stressed state sovereignty and condemned outside interference in internal affairs. At the practical level, Russia has concentrated on developing bilateral relations with the key Asian states: China, India, Japan, and South Korea. Russian leaders no longer characterize U.S. alliances in East Asia as a factor for stability.

Russia's relationship with China is particularly geopolitical. While economic exchange continues to stagnate, political contacts have intensified. In the military area, Moscow has relaxed its arms and technology export controls. After an August 1999 visit to China by Russia's deputy prime minister responsible for the defense industry, a US$2 billion deal was concluded to sell China more than fifty Su-30MKK aircraft. U.S. plans for theater missile defense (TMD) in Northeast Asia and a possible national missile defense (NMD) system in the United States have provided a concrete basis for Russian-Chinese strategic partnership. References to a "Chinese threat" are now more muted in Russia.

Russian-Japanese relations continue on an upward curve, but prospects for a peace treaty in 2000 remain uncertain. The military exchange program was substantially expanded as a result of the August 1999 visit to Russia by the head of Japan's defense agency. Joint naval exercises have been held, and a military hot line established. However, Russia has continuing concerns over the Guidelines for U.S.-Japan Defense Cooperation, which have the effect of making Japan a more active partner in the alliance, the 1999 law on security in areas surrounding Japan, and Japan-U.S. collaboration on TMD.

Relations with the Republic of Korea have recovered from the spy scandal of 1998. President Kim Dae Jung called on Moscow, and the defense ministers of the two countries exchanged visits. In September 1999, Russia offered to sell South Korea six Kilo submarines, following prior sales of tanks and infantry combat vehicles. Moscow welcomes Seoul's Sunshine Policy toward Pyongyang and its cautious approach to TMD. Reciprocating, Russia promised to urge North Korea to take a more conciliatory attitude toward South Korea. However, Moscow's leverage over Pyongyang remains minimal; a new bilateral treaty replacing the 1961 pact contains no clause on military assistance.

In South Asia, Moscow still considers India a long-term strategic partner, as well as the possible basis for a broader strategic partnership including China. Moscow regrets India's new nuclear capability and is seeking ways to stabilize the new nuclear relationship and avert a nuclear conflict, but it has refrained from imposing sanctions. Moscow is paying more attention to Pakistan due to its nuclear status, its hosting of many Islamic militant groups, and the return of the military to power in October. The Pakistani foreign minister made a rare visit to Russia in 1999. Russia is concerned over suspected Pakistani support for Muslim militants in the Caucasus and Central Asia.

DEFENSE POLICIES AND ISSUES

NEW NATIONAL SECURITY CONCEPT   The Kosovo crisis and renewed fighting in the North Caucasus have prompted a major revision of Russia's national security concept. A draft signed in early January 2000 rejects the previous premise that the principal threats to Russia's national security are internal and nonmilitary. Outside intervention—as in Yugoslavia—leading to a possible clash with NATO, militant separatism threatening to tear the country apart—as in the North Caucasus—and international terrorism are now seen as the major dangers to Russia's national security. The document concludes that a new military doctrine is required. The draft also stresses the need for a strong central government in Russia, and calls for increased spending on national security as a whole.

MILITARY DOCTRINE   The Russian military establishment was never happy with the "Fundamentals of Military Doctrine," approved in November 1993, which was seen as vague and naive about global strategic trends. Work on a new document started in 1996, and the draft was presented in early October 1999 even before the new security concept was approved.

The draft acknowledges the decreasing likelihood of a world war, but it concentrates on the rise of nationalist extremism, separatism, local wars, regional arms races, nuclear proliferation, and new security challenges. The reduced role of the United Nations and the Organization for Security and Cooperation in Europe (OSCE), military intervention without a UN Security Council mandate (as in Yugoslavia), and violation of arms control agreements (such as probable U.S. deployment of NMD) are viewed as destabilizing trends. Specific threats include conflicts close to Russia, deployment of foreign military forces on its periphery, and the enlargement of NATO. External threats not necessarily from the West include the training of militants for operations in Russia or allied countries, attacks on Russian military installations, disruption of Russian command and control systems, suppression of the rights and freedoms of Russian citizens, and international terrorism.

Domestic military threats cited are extremism, attacks on infrastructure, illegal armed forces, arms trafficking, and organized crime—all of which are to be found in the North Caucasus. The draft also makes mention of a novel threat, "information expansion," defined as controlling media to sap the nation's morale and patriotism. Massive draft dodging is blamed on this development.

The Russian military believes that, for the most part, threats will require only a limited projection of power within the country and along its immediate continental peripheries. The long-standing aim of parity with the West, whether numerical or qualitative, is now considered unrealistic.

DEFENSE BUDGET   At R105 billion (US$3.81 billion at US$1 = R27.55), Russia's defense spending for the 1999 fiscal year stood at 2.3 percent of the country's GDP, much less than the 3.5 percent promised by President Yeltsin. This continues the trend of requests from the Ministry of Defense being severely trimmed.

Table 1. *Russian Defense Budgets, 1994–1998 (in billions of rubles)*

	1994	1995	1996	1997	1998
Ministry of Defence request	86.5	125.2	160	260	310
Government proposal	37.1	59.4	78.9	100.8	94.5
Final allocation	40.6	59.4	80.2	104.3	99.5

SOURCE: Official government figures.

In 1999, 80 percent of procurement funding went to buy ten Topol-M mobile intercontinental ballistic missiles; twenty to thirty more are to be purchased in 2000. A second regiment of these missiles was expected to be operational by the end of 1999.

In 1999, the military and the government had to find additional funds, amounting to US$37 million, for participation in KFOR and the operations in the North Caucasus. The Dagestan operation in August–September cost R3 billion (US$109 million); estimates for Chechnya vary between R3 billion (US$109 million) and R5 billion (US$181 million). The Caucasus fighting carries an additional penalty: in mid-October, the IMF vowed to stop further disbursement of its loan in order not to be seen as financing Russia's war effort.

NUCLEAR POLICY   Nuclear deterrence remains the mainstay of Russia's defense, requiring the capability to inflict unacceptable damage on the enemy. The new military doctrine retains the option of first use by Russia in response to a large-scale conventional attack. It contemplates limited nuclear war through "non-provoking" strikes. Nonnuclear countries may be targeted if they invade Russia or if they allow their territory to be used for staging an invasion of Russia. Some Russian military thinkers argue in favor of a first-strike strategy; others would reserve the right to use any means, including nuclear weapons, in response to actions undermining Russia's defense capability. An appreciable number of Russian military experts continue to favor the use of tactical nuclear weapons for deterring and parrying regional threats.

The refusal by the U.S. Senate in October 1999 to ratify the Comprehensive Test Ban Treaty (CTBT) and its pending decision on national missile defense have strengthened the hand of the "hawks" in Russia, who see all arms control agreements as essentially unfavorable for Russia. They argue that the numerical limits set by the Strategic Arms Reduction Treaties (START) are too high, the qualitative constraints too narrow, and the resulting structure of strategic forces less than optimal for Russia. Further, the hawks contend, the Intermediate-Range Nuclear Forces (INF) accord has done away with the one means of striking enemy targets on the continent at strategic distances under conditions of enemy air superiority. The Missile Technology Control Regime (MTCR) restricts the competitive advantage of the Russian defense industry as well. Should the Anti-Ballistic Missile (ABM) Treaty be abandoned, the influence of the hawks on Russian foreign and defense policy may grow substantially.

CONVENTIONAL FORCES   No major changes have been announced. Despite Yeltsin's 1996 decree, conscription was not abolished; it is enshrined in the new draft military doctrine. Some two hundred thousand draftees are called up every six months, 60 percent of which serve in the Russian Armed Forces and the remainder in other services such as Interior, Border, Government Communication Agency, and Railroad.

TRAINING AND EQUIPMENT   In 1999, the Russian Armed Forces held military exercises with scenarios based upon the post-Kosovo view of the geostrategic situation. During the "West-99" command post exercise in July, Russia, in alliance with Belarus, was forced to "use" nuclear weapons to defend against a NATO invasion from Poland and across the Baltic States. In a similar exercise in August, forces in the Russian Far East "deployed" nuclear weapons against the United States to stop its open meddling in a conflict between the Russian central government and regional separatists. Planes simulated missile launchings off the coasts of Iceland and Alaska.

The share of the weaponry now considered modern by the Russian Ministry of Defense stands at 25–30 percent of the total. Overall, only 30–60 percent of weapons is in good repair. The Russians consider themselves to be "roughly equal with the world's advanced militaries" in 50–80 percent of research and development, leading in 3–5 percent and trailing in 10–15 percent.

Modernization is the watchword. The Delfin submarine-launched ballistic missile (SLBM) is being modernized. Tu-160 and Tu-95MS heavy bombers—in addition to ten planes to be purchased from Ukraine—are getting a new long-range nonnuclear cruise missile. Modernization is envisaged for Su-27 and Su-30 aircraft, the mainstay of the air force fleet. By 2007, however, acquisition of new weapons will have to start in earnest. The hope is that by then Russia's state finances will have recovered.

DEFENSE INDUSTRY AND ARMS SALES   The defense industry continues to struggle, but it now has hope that with the new military doctrine and with the fighting in the North Caucasus there will be more government orders. The lack of financial resources, however, has led to mounting defense ministry debt to defense contractors, reaching R51 billion (US$1.85 billion) in mid-1999. Selling to foreign customers continues to be the only real source of revenue for firms competing on the world market.

In 1998, Russia sold weapons worth US$2.05 billion to sixty-four states, compared with US$3.5 billion in 1996. Over 80 percent of this trade was with six countries—China, Greece, India, Iran, the United Arab Emirates, and Vietnam; China and India alone accounted for about two-thirds. Of the weapons sold, aircraft and air force equipment comprised about half; army weaponry, about 25 percent; naval ships and equipment, 16 percent; and air defense systems, 8 percent.

Contributions to Global and Regional Security

GLOBAL ARMS CONTROL   Arms control has been directly affected by—and reflects—the deterioration in U.S.-Russian relations. The State Duma had come close to ratifying the 1993 START-2 treaty in December 1998, but it postponed the vote when the United States and Britain launched air raids against Iraq. A second opportunity to ratify START-2 passed in spring 1999 due to the Kosovo situation. Prospects for ratification now depend on how much the new Kremlin leadership will lobby the Duma. The NMD will also be a factor. Russian leaders have been urging the United States to finalize the START-3 treaty, which would correct the flaws of its predecessor. The U.S. Senate, however, has stipulated that Russia must ratify START-2 first.

An even greater challenge to the arms control process looms. Russia's leaders consider the threat to the 1972 ABM Treaty, which represents the cornerstone of strategic stability, as most disturbing. If the United States withdraws from the treaty or decides to deploy NMD, Moscow will think seriously about renouncing the constraints imposed on its strategic nuclear forces by the START-1 and START-2 treaties. Some room for compromise remains, but as with the U.S. Strategic Defense Initiative in the 1980s, Moscow is considering an "asymmetrical response." A worsening of U.S.-Russian strategic relations also threatens the Cooperative Threat Reduction (CTR) program, under which the United States finances the elimination of U.S. and Russian strategic armaments specified in START-1; thus far, US$1.7 billion has been committed to this task, with another US$2.7 billion planned over the next six to seven years.

Having signed but not ratified the CTBT, Russia continues to observe the moratorium on nuclear testing. However, to compensate for lagging behind the United States in laboratory simulation, it has been holding subcritical tests. Continued Russian observance of the moratorium depends on the success of these tests.

Russia's financial difficulties have delayed destruction of chemical weapons. Moscow aims to dispose of its 40,000 tons of poisonous gas by 2009, but only half the necessary funds is currently available.

PEACEKEEPING   Russia continues to contribute to peacekeeping missions, including the multinational effort in the Balkans and independent operations within the former Soviet Union.

Russia's mission with the Stabilization Force (SFOR) in Bosnia continues uneventfully. Russia contributed, with the European Union, to ending the Kosovo crisis, then supported the June 1999 UN Security Council settlement resolution and the KFOR peacekeeping operation. Implementing Russian participation involved hard bargaining and a spectacular march by two hundred Russian paratroopers from Bosnia to Pristina, the capital of Kosovo, consciously risking confrontation with NATO forces. Ultimately, Russia received no sectoral responsibility, its three thousand peacekeepers deployed in other nations' sectors. Moscow continues to oppose strongly what it considers the dismembering of Yugoslavia, and opposes allowing the Kosovo Liberation Army, which it regards as a terrorist organization, to run the province as a separate state.

Russian peacekeeping forces have been in Moldova since 1992. Relations between Moscow and the government of Moldova warmed in 1999. There was a hint that Russia might accelerate military withdrawal from the breakaway territory of Transdniestria, but peace negotiations stalled.

Despite Georgia's unease with Russian peacekeeping operations (although formally a CIS unit) in Abkhazia, and despite its preference for a Western-led force, the status quo persists. Russian troops provide a barrier between the Georgians and the Abkhaz; their departure would likely lead to a resumption of hostilities. Moscow has withdrawn its maritime border force off the Abkhazian coast and relaxed controls on the land border, but it refused to recognize Abkhazian presidential elections in October 1999, which asserted independence from Georgia.

In Tajikistan, the Russian-brokered peace agreement is holding, but the country continues to be torn by clan and regional rivalries, leading to occasional rebellions against the Dushanbe government and the propagation of armed groups not controlled by any authority.

Unlike in 1998, President Yeltsin chose to attend the 1999 summit of the Shanghai Five in Bishkek in August. The forum provided an opportunity to discuss regional security issues—such as Islamic militancy and separatism—and to promote economic exchanges. Moscow made proposals to institutionalize contacts. The primary purpose of this group is to involve China, with Russia's concurrence, as a key player in Central Asia.

REGIONAL   In July 1999, Foreign Minister Igor Ivanov attended a meeting of the ASEAN Regional Forum security dialogue. In September 1999, Russia for the first time participated in the Asia-Pacific Economic Cooperation (APEC) summit as a full member of the group. While Moscow recognizes the weakness of its current position in the region, Russian leaders believe that APEC could be an important long-term vehicle for economic and political involvement in the region.

The situation in East Timor provoked some interest in Russia, which supported the UN Security Council resolution. Moscow was gratified, after Kosovo, to see the Security Council back in action. In its view, however, the peacekeeping operation itself should be the responsibility of regional countries.

15 Singapore

The Security Environment

Singaporeans' perceptions of their security environment in the year 2000 are mixed. There is relief that the consequences of the 1997–1998 Asian economic crisis have not been as dire as feared. There is continuing uncertainty over the future course of Singapore's relations with its closest neighbors. And there is growing confidence both in Singapore's own security capabilities and in Singapore's ability to make at least a modest contribution to strengthening broader regional and global stability.

ECONOMIC RECOVERY   Contrary to the initial projections of Singapore's leaders, developments in 1999 indicated that the worst of the Asian financial crisis was over for most of the region's economies. Singapore's own economy recovered strongly, from 1.5 percent growth in gross national product in 1998 to an estimated 5 percent in 1999 and 6 percent in 2000. Singapore's foreign reserves stood at US$74 billion in June 1999, the world's largest on a per capita basis. Unlike some Southeast Asian countries, Singapore was able to ride out the crisis without domestic instability. This underscored its fundamental strength as well as its lack of internal challenges, such as strong opposition parties, mass protest movements, or separatism.

However, the gradual economic recovery in the region has not necessarily led to a sanguine strategic outlook for Singapore. The second defense minister commented in June that the greatest security challenge for Asia now is how to handle the "hangover" from the crisis. For Singapore, this includes dealing with neighbors that are undergoing difficult political changes, and also improving the image of the Association of Southeast Asian Nations (ASEAN), which has been battered by its inability to deal with the financial crisis or the East Timor issue.

INDONESIA   In February 1999, Senior Minister Lee Kuan Yew warned Singaporeans to be prepared "for more accusations and threats, as leaders of crisis-hit countries such as Indonesia come under more stress in coming months." Lee reaffirmed the importance to Singapore of "rational and stable relations with Indonesia," and stressed that Singapore should "be patient . . . and wait to establish good long-term relations" with whoever emerged as Indonesia's new president.

Nevertheless, Singapore's leadership continued to worry about Indonesia's uncertain trajectory and its potentially negative impact on the city-state. In his February budget speech, Finance Minister Richard Hu stated, "The biggest uncertainty is Indonesia, where social and political tensions threaten to undermine financial and economic reforms. . . . An unsettled Indonesia will color the entire ASEAN region, including Singapore."

Singapore provides important economic benefits to its neighbor. For example, the Singapore-Indonesia gas project in the Natunas Islands is expected to generate revenue of US$8 billion for Indonesia. Also, Singapore contributed humanitarian aid including medicine, rice, and cooking oil to Indonesia during the economic crisis. But Indonesia expects more from its affluent neighbor, while Singapore feels that, as a small country, there is a practical limit to what it can do.

Indonesian President B. J. Habibie remained far from cordial toward Singapore. In February, he alleged that Singapore was a "racist" state that bars Malay citizens from becoming officers in its military. Singapore countered that its military does indeed have ethnic Malay military officers, cautioning Indonesia against interfering in such domestic affairs of a fellow ASEAN country. In July, Habibie advised Singapore "to accept that it was an integrated part of the region. . . . You can never be separated from your shadow. . . . If you want to escape from your shadow and you do not want to unite with your shadow there is only one alternative. You have to live in absolute darkness." To many Singaporeans, these remarks were ominous, reflecting condescension toward a smaller country.

However, there were also bright spots in Singapore-Indonesia relations. The Singapore Armed Forces (SAF) continues to enjoy excellent relations with the Indonesian military. Regular joint land and sea exercises are held, and an airbase at Pekanbaru, Indonesia, is shared. The election in October of Abdurrahman Wahid as Indonesia's president may lead to a friendlier Indonesian disposition and better relations. An early positive sign was a visit by Wahid to Singapore—his first overseas stop—shortly after his election. Singapore, for its part, has sought to mobilize international diplomatic support for Indonesia's territorial integrity.

Nevertheless, Indonesia's road to recovery is likely to be long and arduous, and this is certain to have an effect on Singapore. Should the new Indonesian government fail to improve economic conditions and restore internal stability, religious, ethnic, and regional conflict could trigger outflows of refugees, some of whom might head for Singapore.

MALAYSIA   Singapore's relations with Malaysia are not on an even keel. Defense ties were improved when the annual Five Power Defense Arrangements (FPDA) exercise, which had been canceled by Malaysia in 1998 due in part to its displeasure with Singapore, was held in April 1999. However, other old issues lingered and new irritations appeared.

Both countries agreed to resolve their differences in a comprehensive package, but a diplomatic breakthrough proved elusive. In a holdover from the economic crisis, shares of Malaysian companies traded in Singapore through the Central Limit Order Book (CLOB), valued at S$5.4 billion (US$3.24 billion at S$1 = US$0.60), remained frozen by Kuala Lumpur. Disagreements over the withdrawal of contributions from Singapore's Central Provident Fund by Malaysians, Singapore's relocation of customs, immigration, and quarantine facilities to its Woodlands border checkpoint, and Malaysia's refusal to commit to long-term water supply for Singapore continue to bedevil bilateral relations.

To address the uncertainty of continued water supply, Singapore is seeking to lessen its dependency on others for water. While continuing an active search for the newest and best desalination technology, the government announced plans to build a desalination plant with a capacity of thirty million gallons per day, based on a proven process, by 2005.

Several events in 1999 ruffled bilateral relations. In June, an editorial in Singapore's *Business Times* suggested that Malaysia would be better off with new leadership. This offended Malaysia's leaders, prompting Prime Minister Goh Chok Tong's office to state that the opinion of the *Business Times* was contrary to that of the Singapore government.

The next month, it was Singapore's turn to be offended. After

Singapore announced the planned purchase of Spike missiles from Israel, Malaysian Deputy Defense Minister Abdullah Fadzil Che Wan announced that this did not make him "feel good," and implied that Singapore should be more sensitive toward Islamic feelings in Malaysia about Israel. Singapore's view was that its choices should not be dictated by the sentiments of Kuala Lumpur.

When Singapore revealed plans to redevelop an old Malay palace in Singapore as a Malay Heritage Center, Malaysia's Malay-language press was vehemently critical, charging that this would end "the last symbol of Malay supremacy in the Republic." Singapore Foreign Minister S. Jayakumar lambasted the Malaysian press for "irresponsible and mischievous media reports which amount to interference in our internal affairs . . . [and inflict] possible damage to racial harmony and social stability in Singapore." When *Harakah,* Malaysia's opposition Parti Islam's newspaper, accused Prime Minister Mahathir bin Mohamad of using Singapore to divert attention from domestic issues of "cruelty and corruption" (an allusion to the trial of Mahathir's former deputy Anwar Ibrahim on charges of corruption and sodomy), many Singaporeans agreed.

As the year 2000 began, the leadership of Singapore and its closest neighbor had yet to achieve a stable modus vivendi. Singapore-Malaysia relations are likely to continue to encounter rough patches, due to the burden of history and the memories of Singapore's tumultuous presence and forced exit from Malaysia in the 1960s.

ASEAN   Despite the long-awaited expansion of ASEAN into a ten-country Southeast Asian bloc in 1999, ASEAN's prestige has been severely damaged. Problems include its inability to play an effective role in the Asian financial crisis, squabbling among member countries, semi-anarchy in Indonesia—its largest and pivotal member—and reluctance to get involved in the East Timor issue.

ASEAN did not advocate the cause of freedom and human rights in East Timor because of a general policy of noninterference in members' domestic affairs and because members did not want to offend Indonesia. It was not surprising, therefore, that Australia rather than an ASEAN country became the leader of the International Force in East Timor (INTERFET) peacekeeping operation. ASEAN's international prestige and clout are not likely to be restored until the financial crisis is truly over and Indonesia returns to normalcy and stability. Nevertheless, the ASEAN Regional Forum (ARF) continues to be a useful vehicle, especially for dialogue with major powers and confidence-building measures.

THE GREAT POWERS   Singapore maintains excellent relations with China, Japan, and the United States. The city-state perceives that a stable China-Japan-U.S. relationship is vital to the region. Deputy Prime Minister and First Defense Minister Tony Tan stated, "We were very fortunate in the last two years when the economic crisis was at its height, the [China-Japan-U.S.] relationship was stable and the United States and China had a good relationship. This provided crucial stability to the region."

Recent developments involving both China and the United States should bolster long-term regional stability. Beijing for the first time agreed to ASEAN's proposal to discuss a code of conduct for claimant states in the South China Sea. It also agreed in principle to ratify the ASEAN-proposed Southeast Asian Nuclear-Weapons-Free Zone—setting a precedent for other nuclear powers, especially the United States and India, and improving prospects for establishment of the zone. The U.S. naval presence, reflecting the U.S. commitment to maintaining the strategic balance in the region, will be facilitated by access for U.S. ships, including aircraft carriers, to Singapore's new Changi Naval Base.

DEFENSE POLICIES AND ISSUES

POLICY   As a small city-state with an acute sense of vulnerability in an uncertain Asia Pacific, Singapore strives to maintain credible deterrence by staying at the technological cutting edge in the region, thereby compensating for its small manpower base and lack of strategic depth.

The Asian financial crisis showed how quickly an environment that appeared stable can take a turn for the worse, and that Singapore can never take regional peace and security for granted. An October 1999 Ministry of Defense submission to Parliament stressed: "[The] need to maintain strong defense will require steady investments in both good times and bad. The SAF has developed into a well-balanced, integrated and technologically advanced fighting force. . . . The SAF will benchmark itself against the best armed forces in the world and continually refine our training procedures and methodology [and] increasingly utilize simulation technology to provide realistic and cost-effective training locally."

DEFENSE SPENDING   In fiscal year 1999, defense spending accounted for 24.9 percent of the Singapore government budget—S$7,270 million (US$4.36 billion). Of this total, S$6,650 million (US$3,990 million) was allocated to operating expenditure (salaries, maintenance, and equipment), and S$620 million (US$372 million) to development expenditure (development and renovation of camps).

PERSONNEL AND TRAINING   According to the International Institute for Strategic Studies, in 1999 the SAF comprised 72,500 personnel (including 39,800 conscripts) and more than 250,000 reserves. Although the SAF is predominantly a conscript and reservist army, the rising educational level of the average rank-and-file soldier in Singapore means that the SAF is able to absorb and maintain increasingly sophisticated weapons systems.

In 1999, American defense analysts ranked the Republic of Singapore Navy (RSN) as the best naval force in the region, ahead of larger and older Southeast Asian fleets. In response, Singapore's *Straits Times* commented, "This reaffirms what is acknowledged in international defense circles—that the SAF is the superior military force in the region in terms of professionalism, operational capability, war-fighting hardware and manpower qualities."

Although the SAF is a professional, high-technology force, it lacks combat experience. To compensate, the SAF seeks to train with and learn from the military of friendly countries that have experienced combat and are also technologically advanced. In recent years, Singapore has energetically expanded security ties, sought foreign bases for training, and acquired sophisticated weapons systems from various countries. This "globalization" and the development of an indigenous arms industry are possible because Singapore has both the financial resources and the skilled manpower to support such a strategy.

DOMESTIC TECHNOLOGY AND PRODUCTION   To better harness technology to maintain its strategic edge, the defense ministry has streamlined its organization and is currently restructuring its technology arm, the Defense Technology Group (DTG). The ministry will concentrate on giving strategic direction, while technical functions are devolved to the new Defense Science and Technology Agency (DSTA). This restructuring was to be completed by April 2000.

The DSO (Defense Science Organization) National Laboratory now has more than five hundred scientists and engineers working on such technologies as protection against toxic chemicals, "spin analysis" for fighter aircraft, robotics, and electronic warfare systems.

The indigenous arms industry has also made significant progress. In 1999, the Singapore Assault Rifle (SAR21) was officially unveiled. It is smaller, lighter, easier to maintain, and more accurate than the American-designed M16, which it will replace. It is the first rifle in the world to have a built-in laser aiming device for night firing, and has a magnifying optical scope for greater accuracy.

The RSN's new tank landing ships are also domestically built; the fourth is scheduled for delivery in 2001. The role of these ships is to transport personnel and equipment to overseas training areas. The RSN is now planning a new class of warship with radar-evading stealth capabilities. Four-to-six stealth corvettes will replace the navy's current missile gunboats, with the first expected to enter service in 2004–2005.

The Republic of Singapore Air Force (RSAF) has upgraded its fleet of old F-5E/Fs to F-5S with advanced avionics. The forty upgraded aircraft will enjoy an extra ten-year life span, with new radar, weapons delivery, navigation system, and computerized cockpit controls reputed to be comparable to those of the F-16. This upgrading also reflects the domestic aerospace industry's technological expertise.

FOREIGN PROCUREMENT AND COOPERATION The SAF acquires weapons systems abroad when it lacks the technological expertise or when it is not economical to build them domestically. However, such purchases are spread among a number of countries, in order to obtain the most suitable systems for Singapore and to avoid dependence on a single supplier. The SAF has announced the following foreign purchases:

- From the United States: A US$620 million package that includes eight Apache attack helicopters, 216 Hellfire-II laser-guided missiles, 120 Hydra-70 rockets, spare parts, communications equipment, training, and technical support; CH-47 Chinook helicopters, reputed to be one of the world's most versatile long-range heavy-utility helicopters (three out of six are expected to be deployed in Singapore); and four KC-135 jet tankers able to refuel RSAF fighter aircraft in midair and to ferry SAF troops and equipment for overseas training exercises.

- From Sweden: Sjoormen-class submarines; RSS *Conqueror* and RSS *Centurion* launched by RSN at the Kockums Shipyard in Kaiskrona, Sweden; four others expected to be operational by 2001–2002 and based at the new Changi Naval Base.
- A Russian-made Igla surface-to-air missile (SAM) system.
- From Israel: Spike missiles.

On June 16, Singapore and France signed a General Security Agreement that covers the exchange of classified information and facilitates defense technology cooperation and other mutually beneficial interaction between the two countries. Also in 1999, the RSAF's Helicopter Detachment in Oakey, Queensland, was officially opened. This facility, costing A$20 million (US$13 million at A$1 = US$0.65), supports twelve super Puma helicopters and 160 RSAF personnel.

The RSAF now benefits from training space and facilities in Bangladesh, Brunei, France, Indonesia, New Zealand, South Africa, and the United States, as well as Australia. These arrangements also enable the RSAF to benchmark itself against some of the longer-established and most technologically advanced air forces in the world.

CONTRIBUTIONS TO REGIONAL AND GLOBAL STABILITY

The 1997–1998 Asian financial crisis demonstrated that a collapse of regional economic prosperity could trigger regional strategic and political instability. Thus, it is in Singapore's own self-interest to contribute to the economic prosperity of the region, because this also enhances regional stability.

Singapore actively supports the rule of international law and global and regional institutions—especially the United Nations, ASEAN, and the ARF—as indispensable to its survival and prosperity. Singapore contributes to the UN Iraq-Kuwait Observation Mission. It contributed 250 medical and logistics personnel to the INTERFET mission in East Timor, and two RSN tank landing craft transport supplies and equipment between Darwin and Dili. Singapore is seeking election to a nonpermanent UN Security Council seat in 2001; if elected, it intends to work to strengthen the role of the Security Council.

Singapore wants to move the ARF from confidence building toward preventive diplomacy in order to further strengthen regional stability and peace. Singapore is preparing a paper on the concept and principles of preventive diplomacy for discussion at the spring 2000 ARF senior officials' meeting.

Singapore believes that its provision of air force and naval facilities to the United States helps maintain strategic balance and stability in Asia Pacific. It is also committed to the Five Power Defense Arrangements, the only multilateral defense agreement in the region. In 1999, the Singapore army and the U.S. army in the Pacific cohosted the 23rd Pacific Armies Management Seminar and the inaugural Pacific Armies Chiefs Conference in Singapore.

In 1999, Prime Minister Goh initiated the East-Asia Latin American Forum (Ealaf), which links Asia and Latin America, after having previously launched the Asia-Europe Meeting (ASEM) forum. The rationale was that while the United States, Europe, and Asia have strong ties, there is a "missing link" between Asia and Latin America. Ealaf will fill the gap by bringing together at least twenty-seven countries from the two regions. If successful, Ealaf will enhance economic, cultural, and political ties among the member countries. Singapore and Chile will coordinate the first two sets of meetings, aiming for an Ealaf gathering of foreign ministers in 2001.

China and Japan, the two East Asian powers, will participate in Ealaf; the United States will not, as it does not participate in the ASEM meetings. One Japanese newspaper speculated that "against the backdrop of the Asian financial crisis . . . [Ealaf] hopes to strengthen the voices of these countries against the United States, the IMF [International Monetary Fund], and other world organizations." If ASEM and Ealaf develop successfully, this would also mean that it is possible for even a tiny city-state to make a significant contribution to international relations.

16 Thailand

In 2000, Thailand is still recovering from the 1997–1998 economic crisis even as it implements controversial political and military reforms. Thais see no threat of a major war in the next decade, but remain concerned over problems along Thailand's borders, particularly with Myanmar. Thailand seeks good relations with its neighbors and all the major powers, and is working to revitalize the Association of Southeast Asian Nations (ASEAN) and to support regional and global security building processes.

INTERNAL   *The Economy.* Thailand's gross domestic product is projected to grow by 3–4 percent in 1999, compared to a contraction of 9.4 percent in 1998. Other positive signs include growth in exports and domestic consumption and a surge in manufacturing. Policies implemented since 1998 include tax cuts, capital support, stimulation of the real estate sector, and financial restructuring for small- and medium-scale industries. Public-sector reforms emphasize fiscal decentralization, privatization, and improvement in administrative efficiency. In September 1999, the government announced that foreign exchange reserves had risen sufficiently such that withdrawals under the International Monetary Fund (IMF) program would no longer be necessary.

Nevertheless, the economy still faces problems. Investment is declining, and the banking system is strapped by significant nonperforming loans. Unemployment has continued to rise, reaching 1.87 million or 5.65 percent of the 33.08 million workforce in mid-1999, as compared with 1.5 percent in 1997 and 4 percent at the end of 1998. According to official surveys, 7.9 million Thais, about 13 percent of the population, were living in poverty at the end of 1998, an increase from 6.8 million, or 11.4 percent, before the economic crisis.

Domestic Politics. Economic recovery measures have at the same time created internal problems for Prime Minister Chuan Leekpai. Critics blame his administration for an economic policy that has expanded public debt while ignoring the real sector, and that has chosen to sell national assets to foreigners. The fiercest opposition to economic policy has come from people who have been most directly affected, such as state enterprise workers.

The 1997 constitution generated high public expectation for political reform. Legislatively, however, beneficiaries of the status quo and advocates of reform have struggled over the terms of reform, and many of the new mechanisms for transparency in government are yet to function effectively. Activists have charged that change has been inadequate, and they have again turned to protests. Some call for the dissolution of parliament, in the hope that a revised electoral system will produce a new breed of politicians.

Insurgency. Insurgent violence in South Thailand has largely subsided, as a result of cooperation from Kuala Lumpur and a 1998 amnesty to insurgents who give up armed struggle. In September 1999, the government issued a new security policy for the five southern provinces, emphasizing human resource development and respect for local customs, thus enabling the local Muslim majority to live without fear within Thai society.

CROSS-BORDER ISSUES   Thailand's 2,630-kilometer land border and 5,656-kilometer sea boundary continue to be a source of differences between Thailand and its neighbors. Most of the border issues are being managed in a relatively peaceful manner, but Thailand's border with Myanmar has been the scene of more serious problems.

Drug Trafficking. Drug trafficking is a major issue. The ethnic Burmese Wa's United Wa State Army (UWSA), one of the largest armed drug-trafficking groups in the world, commanding some 20,000 troops, operates out of Myanmar's Shan state, next door to Thailand's northern provinces. Thai forces and the UWSA have clashed often. The northeast region of Thailand has also become a major drug route, with several large production facilities along the Lao border.

With the death penalty for drug dealing in Malaysia and Singapore, drug traffickers have brought more of their business intoThailand. In recent years, Malaysians have constituted the largest number of drug dealers arrested in Thailand. However, critics also point to inefficiency and corruption in law enforcement.

The government implemented a series of drastic antidrug measures in 1999. The Money Laundering Control Act of 1999 aims at cutting the financial lifeline of drug traffickers. The army has been assigned to antidrug duty in seven northern provinces, and heavily armed soldiers are stationed at major checkpoints along the Myanmar border. There have been periodic border closures, reportedly to the displeasure of Yangon.

Illegal Workers and Refugees. Since the economic crisis, more than one million illegal workers, mostly from Myanmar, and some one hundred thousand Myanmar refugees have entered Thailand. The security establishment regards these inflows as a threat to Thai stability, and in 1999 it launched a vigorous campaign against hiring foreign workers.

In early August, the government issued a regulation that only 162,000 foreign workers would be allowed to remain in the country after November 3. Starting in October, thousands of illegal immigrants were deported. This action, however, soon met with complications. Contending that members of dissident groups were among the deported workers, Myanmar troops threatened to shoot deported workers. Yangon would not negotiate with Bangkok over the issue. Thai factory owners, in addition, threatened mass protests over the deportations, and large numbers of deported workers found ways to return to Thailand. Nevertheless, in November the government reaffirmed the policy.

There have been other incidents with Myanmar refugees, in particular cross-border attacks by pro-Yangon Karens on the mostly anti-Yangon Karens in border camps. In August, Thailand relocated these camps to an area less vulnerable to attacks, and Bangkok has asked the United Nations High Commissioner for Refugees (UNHCR) to negotiate with Yangon for the refugees' repatriation.

THAILAND-MYANMAR RELATIONS   The relationship between Bangkok and Yangon is a difficult one. Progress on border demarcation has been very limited, and confrontations over disputed areas both on land and at sea have been frequent. In early 1999, a series of incursions into Thai territory by armed groups from Myanmar prompted the Thai military commander to threaten strong counteraction.

In March, Prime Minister Chuan and Myanmar Prime Minister General Than Shwe met in Thailand to discuss drug trafficking and border issues. However, the meeting produced only an agreement for further consultation on border issues and the formation of a joint committee to study the drug problem.

With increased democratization in Thailand, the differences between the political systems of Thailand and Myanmar have further complicated relations. When armed Myanmar dissidents seized the Myanmar embassy in Bangkok in October 1999, a senior Thai minister referred to the dissidents as "students who are fighting for democracy." Thais generally approved of the government's handling of this incident, which was to arrange for the peaceful surrender of the perpetrators in exchange for safe passage out of Thailand. Yangon expressed its dissatisfaction with these terms by closing its Thai border checkpoints and canceling fishing licenses for Thai vessels. In the past, such tactics sometimes produced changes in Thai policy as affected businesses pressed their interests upon the government, but factors such as human rights now carry more weight in Thai policy making. Thus, despite the government's attempt to avoid further incident by asking the UNHCR to resettle the 2,800 anti-Yangon students from Thai refugee camps in third countries, the situation with Myanmar remains volatile.

RELATIONS WITH OTHER NEIGHBORS *Laos.* The regional economic crisis had a negative effect on Thailand-Laos relations. Due to reduced demand for electricity, Thailand sought a delay in purchases of electricity from hydroelectric projects in Laos and a lower price. As these changes would harm the Lao economy, Vientiane called on Bangkok to honor the original agreement.

On the positive side, Bangkok acted to remove anti-Vientiane Hmong refugees from their longtime stronghold in Saraburi province. Through the UNHCR, the remaining 1,600 Laotians in the camp were to be repatriated by the end of 1999.

Cambodia. Thailand-Cambodia relations had long been strained over Phnom Penh's belief that Thailand supported the Khmer Rouge, but with the collapse of the Khmer Rouge in 1998 cooperation between the two countries has improved. In June 1999, the first meeting of the Thai-Cambodian Joint Commission on Land Boundary Demarcation agreed to start work on the 798-kilometer border. This task will not be easy, because the border area has extensive minefields, and most border markers have disappeared or been moved. However, the United States and Japan have offered assistance in de-mining the area, and during a visit by Thailand's supreme commander to Phnom Penh in October, the two governments agreed to form joint de-mining teams. Thailand's Ministry of Defense is also planning a military training assistance program in Cambodia.

Malaysia. In August, the Thai-Malaysian Joint Commission discussed cooperation against illegal activities such as the smuggling of narcotics, women, and children. The governments also agreed to construct a second bridge at the Kolok River, open a new border checkpoint, and form a Thai-Malaysian Business Council.

Vietnam. In June, the Thai and Vietnamese navies implemented the first phase of an agreement to prevent incidents in the Gulf of Thailand where there are areas of overlapping claims, establishing radio communication between the two commands. In October, joint patrols began along the 4,840-square kilometer disputed area.

THE MAJOR POWERS   *China.* Diplomatic relations between Thailand and China further improved in 1999. In February, the two countries signed a comprehensive cooperation plan for the twenty-first century, a first for China. During an April visit by Prime Minister Chuan to China, an agreement was signed establishing a joint committee to study prospects for Chinese investment in Thailand. China also extended special preferences for the purchase of Thai agricultural products.

Chinese President Jiang Zemin visited Thailand in September. The Thai and Chinese people are "like brothers," he stated, and in the first visit by a foreign head of state to Bangkok's two-century-old Chinatown, he called on the Thai-Chinese community to help strengthen ties between Beijing and Bangkok.

President Jiang also stated that Thailand was China's closest and oldest ally in Southeast Asia, clearly hoping that these ties would contribute to better relations with other ASEAN members. Jiang reiterated that a developed China would not pose a threat to any country. He supported ASEAN's efforts to establish a zone of peace, freedom, and neutrality, as well as the Southeast Asian Nuclear-Weapons-Free Zone, signaling that China was ready to hold discussions with the relevant ASEAN countries on the South China Sea.

Nevertheless, Thai security officials are not completely comfortable with China's military policies. Thai military leaders have publicly expressed their concern at Yangon's acquisition of new weapons at "friendship prices" from "superpowers"—an apparent reference to China, which is a major weapons supplier to Myanmar. A committee commissioned by the Ministry of Defense to review the changing security situation in the region identified China's military policy as one of the factors that should be closely monitored.

The United States. The United States remains a major security partner. The annual "Cobra Gold" Thai-U.S. military exercise was one of the largest conducted by the U.S. Pacific Command in 1999, involving 6,300 U.S. personnel and 12,000 Thai troops. In August, the first de-mining course began under the U.S.-funded Humanitarian Assistance and De-mining Program. During a visit to Bangkok in October, U.S. Secretary of Defense William Cohen commended the Thai government for participating in the International Force in East Timor (INTERFET), and offered U.S. logistics assistance and training for Thai peacekeeping forces. In addition, the two countries continue a wide range of cooperative antidrug activities.

However, political and public relations between the two countries are strained. Geopolitical changes have produced a divergence in national interests and policy. For example, Thailand characterized the bombing of the Chinese embassy in Belgrade in May 1999 as "a clear violation of international law," maintaining that Beijing deserved an explanation and compensation. Bangkok also urged the UN Security Council to find a solution to the Kosovo crisis.

The economic crisis soured Thai public attitudes toward the United States. Some believed Americans were responsible for the crisis, some complained that the United States had been slow in giving assistance, while others believed the "U.S.-led" IMF program only opened the way for American domination of the Thai economy.

For much of 1999, Thai attention focused on the role of the United States in the protracted selection process for the head of the World Trade Organization (WTO). U.S. opposition to the Thai candidate was generally regarded as unfair and deceitful. An opinion poll showed extraordinarily high resentment against the United States, and politicians urged the government to reexamine its relations with the United States. The government remained publicly reserved, but Bangkok's tough diplomatic dealing with Washington on the WTO issue was demonstration of its independence.

Japan. Thailand's relations with Japan remain excellent. Japan is the biggest donor to the IMF fund for Thailand, and it provided a concessional loan of B53 billion (US$1.41 billion at US$1 = B37.5) through its Miyazawa Fund, which was established in 1998 to assist Southeast Asian economies suffering from the economic crisis. A fund-supported social development program launched in April promoted economic stimulation through short-term employment. The program is viewed positively by the public. Bangkok also greatly appreciated Tokyo's vigorous diplomatic support for the Thai candidate for the WTO leadership.

DEFENSE POLICIES AND ISSUES

The commander of Thailand's army inceasingly emphasizes the army's role in supporting national development. This includes emergency relief and suppression of illegal drugs—roles considered suitable because of the army's engineering equipment and trained personnel. The commander also advocates active Thai opposition to genocide, ethnic cleansing, and human rights violations around the world, and believes the Thai army should be prepared to participate in international peacekeeping operations.

DEFENSE SPENDING   The defense budget for fiscal year 2000 is B77.3 billion (US$2.0 billion), an increase of 0.3 percent from 1999. This is approximately 9.3 percent of the total government budget and 1.43 percent of GDP. Defense received the third largest allocation after the education and interior ministries.

In August 1999, for the first time since the economic crisis, the government approved a major defense purchase of twenty-five secondhand Alpha jets from Germany, costing B1,250 billion (US$33.3 million). The new planes are for reconnaissance purposes and will replace obsolete aircraft.

RESTRUCTURING   The government is seeking a more streamlined, efficient, and modernized military. The Ministry of Defense has been preparing a highly ambitious restructuring plan for 2000–2007. The major elements are as follows:
- Restructuring of the Ministry of Defense. This includes changes in both the chain of command and the administrative structure. Some combat units will be disbanded, and some activities privatized.
- Downsizing the armed forces. Manpower will be reduced by a total of 72,215 positions (17 percent). Headquarters staff will be cut by 5,000 positions (15 percent), the army 37,512 (15 percent), the navy 17,845 (17.5 percent), and the air force 11,858 (21.5 percent).
- Reduced procurement. The naval combat fleet will be reduced from

81 to 77 vessels, minesweepers from 30 to 22, and aircraft from 102 to 98. Air force squadrons will be reduced from 36 to 24, and air bases from 26 to 20. New purchases will be to replace existing aircraft.

TRANSPARENCY   The plan to increase transparency within the armed forces, implementing the 1997 constitution, has been accelerated. A proposed freedom of information law will make it difficult for the armed forces to maintain exclusive control over military information. The 1997 charter also affects the privileges and commercial activities, including broadcasting, of the armed forces. Despite resistance from some officers, this process is moving ahead.

CONTRIBUTIONS TO REGIONAL AND GLOBAL SECURITY

REGIONAL SECURITY: ASEAN   The Thai government places high priority on maintaining ASEAN solidarity and revitalizing the association.

Thailand lobbied intensely to get ASEAN-EU exchanges back on track after almost two years of wrangling over the status of Myanmar in ASEAN-EU forums. The European Union's sanctions against Myanmar led to the cancellation of an ASEAN-EU meeting of foreign ministers scheduled for early 1999 in Berlin, and delayed for almost a year and a half the 13th ASEAN–European Commission Joint Cooperation Committee (JCC). The JCC meeting was finally held in May in Bangkok, with Myanmar present as a passive participant.

In June, Thailand and seven other ASEAN members voted against an International Labor Organization (ILO) resolution condemning forced labor in Myanmar and cutting off all ILO assistance to Myanmar. The opposition was led by Thai officials, who believed the resolution would further harm Thai credibility with major trade partners critical of Thai labor standards and practices.

In August 1999, Thailand assumed the chairmanship of ASEAN. Foreign Minister Surin Pitsuwan stated that, in order to make ASEAN "a center of gravity," member countries must recognize and manage their differences in levels of development and political systems. He called for assistance to Cambodia, Laos, Myanmar, and Vietnam in infrastructure and human resource development. He argued that it is unnecessary for members to agree on every issue, because political systems differ and outsiders can do little to alter other countries' domestic politics.

Rather, he said members should address individually their own domestic and regional concerns. Surin's statement was a formulation that departed somewhat from the concept of "flexible engagement" that he had proposed in 1998, which allowed members to express their views on internal developments in other ASEAN countries that affected the association as a whole; "flexible engagement" had drawn strong opposition from some ASEAN members, including Myanmar and Indonesia.

Even so, Bangkok's "flexible" approach was reflected in its decision in September to contribute 1,500 soldiers to the UN-organized INTERFET, and to provide the deputy commander of the force. The government argued that the East Timor issue had become the most severe security problem in the region, that there was an urgent need to restore peace, that absent an ASEAN mandate it was appropriate for the issue to be handled within the UN framework, and that Indonesia had approved the force.

The INTERFET decision aroused domestic opposition. Critics argued that it further burdened the country's budget and that it was a pro-U.S. policy harmful to Thai relations with Indonesia. In response, the army commander strongly defended Thai participation in INTERFET, citing the moral obligation to prevent crimes against humanity, Thailand's economic interest in regional stability, and Thailand's duty as a member of the United Nations.

GLOBAL SECURITY   Although Thailand's major security contributions are in Southeast Asia, it also participates in peacekeeping and security-building efforts around the world. In 1999, simultaneous with INTERFET, Thailand contributed troops to a UN Observer Mission to Sierra Leone in the aftermath of a civil war. In May, the foreign minister attended a meeting organized by Canada and Norway on strengthening international cooperation in such matters as international humanitarian laws and human rights.

17 The United States

THE SECURITY ENVIRONMENT

The United States entered the year 2000—an election year and the last year of the Clinton presidency—with less clarity or certainty in the security environment than at any time in the post–cold war decade. Domestic debate continues over the international role of the United States and related defense policy issues. Globally, some analysts fear the emergence of a new bipolarity, as Russia and China both opposed the U.S.-led NATO (North Atlantic Treaty Organization) intervention in Kosovo. In the Asia Pacific region, particular concerns are U.S.-China relations and the complex U.S.-China-Japan triangular relationship, as well as the traditional flashpoints of the Korean peninsula and the Taiwan Strait. In 1999, different combinations of interests and circumstances produced differing U.S. responses in situations such as Kosovo, North Korea, and East Timor.

DOMESTIC INFLUENCES   The post–cold war domestic debate over the appropriate U.S. international role continues. No new consensus has emerged to replace the certitudes of the cold war era.
   Policy Differences. The principal division is between international/multilateral and national/unilateral approaches to foreign and security policy. A related issue is the desirable degree of leadership and involvement of the United States in world problems. Isolationism is a more minor factor. Views such as opposition to the United Nations are actually more unilateralist—reflecting the belief that the United States, as the sole superpower, can and should have its own way. The unilateralist view does not reject letting others take the lead, especially if this reduces

U.S. costs or if the focus is in an area of less direct U.S. concern. But it emphasizes that the United States should not permit its interests to be blocked or compromised by international institutions or regimes, and that the United States should act unilaterally if necessary—for example, in imposing sanctions or punishment on offending governments. The multilateralist approach puts much greater emphasis on building international consensus, taking account of other perspectives, and acting through multilateral institutions.

Process and Politics. The fundamental policy debate is complicated by several factors relating to process. There are differences of view within the administration, within Congress, and within the political parties, as well as between the administration and Congress, and among elite and public opinion. Larger policy issues usually arise in the context of specific situations, which tend to be complex and on which expert opinion is often divided. Furthermore, in the post–cold war period there has been increased partisanship in foreign policy, particularly when different parties have controlled the Congress and the executive branch. In an election year, politics can be even more complicated, but foreign policy is not usually the major focus of presidential campaigns. Thus, the debate is complicated, and results may be uneven and confusing.

The Economy. Absent an economic shock, neither domestic nor international economic issues appear likely to affect American security perceptions significantly in 2000. Basic U.S. economic trends remain strongly positive, with a record period of economic expansion as of February 2000; growth continued at approximately 4 percent in 1999, with inflation and unemployment both very low. However, record and still-growing trade deficits, in which Asian countries have a major share, still have the potential to cause complications in U.S. relations with Asia Pacific trade partners.

ASIA PACIFIC   The Asia Pacific region is a major factor in the U.S. security equation, with as much of America's security forces dedicated to this region as to Europe. American consciousness of the region is somewhat episodic and tends to focus on specific subregions and issues, but it is growing. A national opinion survey sponsored by the Henry Luce Foundation in mid-1999 found indications of increasing public recognition of the importance of Asia Pacific to the United States. Majorities view China, Japan, and Russia as of "vital interest" to the United States, and favor keeping U.S. forces in Japan and South Korea and defending those allies if necessary. Notably, the survey found that a majority of the public ranks China as "primarily a threat" to the United States.

U.S.-China Relations. In 1999, the Sino-American relationship was sorely tried. The year began with harsh Chinese criticism of possible U.S.-Japan cooperation in theater missile defense (TMD), and with American accusations of Chinese nuclear espionage. The visit of Premier Zhu Rongji to the United States in April, undertaken at some political risk for Zhu given the tenor of the relationship, failed to achieve the primary Chinese objective (and Zhu's expectation) of agreement on terms for Chinese entry into the World Trade Organization (WTO). Embarrassment turned to outrage after the accidental U.S. bombing of the Chinese embassy in Belgrade in early May during the NATO Kosovo campaign, prompting violent demonstrations at the U.S. embassy and other posts in China. Conversely, the release in late May by the U.S. Congress of the "Cox Report" on Chinese nuclear spying served to reinforce American suspicions of China.

Official relations were put back on a more normal track after a meeting between U.S. President Bill Clinton and Chinese President Jiang Zemin at the Asia-Pacific Economic Cooperation (APEC) summit in September, and after the two countries reached a long-elusive WTO agreement in November. However, toward the end of the year, the Chinese crackdown on the Falun Gong spiritual movement and other events relating to Tibet and freedom of speech brought renewed attention to China human rights issues in U.S. public opinion. The outlook for U.S.-China relations in 2000 is highly uncertain.

U.S.-Japan Relations. In contrast with U.S.-China relations, developments in U.S.-Japan security relations and cooperation in 1999 were generally quite positive. In May, the Japanese Diet passed legislation implementing the new Guidelines for U.S.-Japan Defense Cooperation agreed in September 1997, and in August the two governments signed an agreement on cooperation in research on a TMD system. Both actions were spurred by Japanese concern over the potential threat to Japan from North Korean missile development. At the end of the year, there was a breakthrough in the long-stalled effort to relocate Futenma Air Station on Okinawa to a less populous area of the island.

Problems remain in all these areas, however. Certain aspects of the guidelines, such as when and where Japan might participate in inspecting foreign ships, were left unclear and could again raise political sensitivities within Japan. There have been suggestions that Japan might want to develop an independent missile defense capability and differences over policy toward North Korea. And the question of relocating the Okinawa bases is far from settled—with the prefectural government seeking an end to the bases by 2015 and the potential for disruption of the Group of Eight economic summit meeting scheduled to be held in Okinawa in July 2000.

The North Korea and Taiwan Factors. Developments in the critical trilateral relationship between the United States, China, and Japan have been significantly affected by actions taken by North Korea. Pyongyang's threat to conduct another multistage missile test (following on the test of August 1998 that overflew Japan), combined with the discovery in August 1998 of construction of a large new underground facility in North Korea, renewed U.S. and Japanese (as well as South Korean) concerns about North Korean intentions. The latest crisis was eventually resolved through a U.S.–North Korea agreement in September 1999 freezing North Korean missile testing in return for the lifting of some economic sanctions by the United States, coupled with an inspection of the underground facility that produced no evidence of nuclear activity.

In October, former U.S. Defense Secretary William Perry released the report of a yearlong study of policy toward North Korea that attempted to address the overall problem. Perry recommended a dual strategy, offering normalized political and economic relations in return for a continued North Korean freeze on nuclear weapon and missile development, while also maintaining a deterrent capability including U.S. troops stationed in South Korea. Perry's recommendations were favorably received in Seoul and Tokyo. However, this rare consensus could be threatened by renewed North Korean brinkmanship or by opposition from conservative elements in South Korea and the U.S. Congress who view this approach as rewarding a tyrannical regime.

In the meantime, the U.S.-Japan agreement to cooperate on missile defense in response to the North Korean threat only exacerbated Chinese objections to TMD development. The primary Chinese concern was over possible TMD coverage of Taiwan. Tensions between China and Taiwan were further heightened by Taiwan President Lee Teng-hui's statement in July that Taiwan-China relations should be on a "state-to-state" basis. This prompted strong protests by China, an increase in military activity on both sides of the Strait, and the postponement of a planned visit to Taiwan by China's cross-Strait negotiator. These renewed tensions seem likely to persist through the Taiwanese presidential elections in March 2000. The U.S. presidential election year also invites partisan position taking in support of democratic Taiwan and opposing human rights–violating China. The vicious circle of mutual mistrust and countermoves has the potential for miscalculation, accidents, and further escalation of tensions.

Russia. Like U.S.-China relations, U.S.-Russia relations were also strained as 2000 began. The deterioration of the relationship was due primarily to developments in Europe and the Persian Gulf area— especially Kosovo, Iraq, and Iran—rather than the Asia Pacific. It was compounded at year-end by the resignation of Russian President Boris Yeltsin and his handover of power to Vladimir Putin, the architect of the second war in Chechnya that was openly criticized by the U.S. administration.

The deterioration of U.S.-Russia relations has the potential to affect the security situation in Asia Pacific in several ways. Closer cooperation with China is a logical strategy for Russia that could have the effect of hardening Chinese attitudes toward the United States and the West. Russian refusal to renegotiate the Anti-Ballistic Missile Treaty, which would be necessary if the United States is to deploy advanced missile defenses without violating the treaty's terms, assists China in its effort to prevent U.S.-Japanese development of TMD. Russia has also sold arms and technology to Beijing. The net impact is impossible to predict but, if combined with other disruptive developments, could be profound.

Southeast Asia and South Asia. Outbreaks of conflict in Indonesia and between India and Pakistan were the primary focus of attention during 1999. Southeast Asia seemed to be on the road to recovery from the economic crisis that had greatly concerned American policymakers and analysts a year earlier. However, Indonesia was an exception. There, continuing economic crisis was compounded by political volatility exacerbated by national and presidential elections and by the conflict following the East Timor referendum on independence, which led to the UN-backed peacekeeping intervention in September.

U.S. officials have consistently urged the Indonesian government to continue the processes of economic and political reform. At the same time, the United States strongly criticized Indonesia's failure to ensure security in East Timor and pressured Indonesia to accept the UN peacekeeping force, INTERFET (International Force in East Timor), to which it contributed support personnel. The advent of the Abdurrahman Wahid government in October was welcomed in Washington as a hopeful development, opening possibilities for improved political consensus and reform. However, serious challenges, including a secessionist movement in Aceh province, pose major questions for the stability of this linchpin Southeast Asian country.

In South Asia, the incursion of Pakistani forces into the Indian-controlled Kargil sector of Kashmir in May–July, followed by the military takeover in Pakistan in October, added to uncertainties caused by the nuclear testing by both nations in 1998. U.S.-Pakistan relations were further strained by the Kargil situation, and U.S. officials engaged in blunt exchanges with Pakistani counterparts. Meanwhile, the high-level dialogue with India begun after the 1998 nuclear tests continued. Although no breakthroughs on nuclear issues seemed likely, the planned visit by President Clinton to India in March 2000 offered an opportunity for further warming in U.S.-India relations.

DEFENSE POLICIES AND ISSUES

DOCTRINE   The most current comprehensive statement of U.S. security policy regarding the Asia Pacific region remains "The United States Security Strategy for the East Asia-Pacific Region," issued at the end of 1998. By the end of 1999, evolving conditions in Asia Pacific had rendered the rather optimistic 1998 assessment—with its emphasis on continuity in U.S. regional relationships and engagement, including the commitment to the forward deployment of 100,000 troops—increasingly outdated. However, neither legislation nor administration policy required a formal policy review. And, as usual, U.S. policymakers were preoccupied with concerns elsewhere: the Kosovo problem and intervention, NATO's fiftieth anniversary summit in April, which saw the admission of three former Soviet allies and the issuance of a new, post–cold war NATO strategic concept, and developments in the Middle East and South Asia.

However, the process of adapting service doctrines and force structures to anticipated missions continued. For example, in October 1999 the army unveiled a plan—to be implemented over a period of years—for lighter, more mobile fighting units suitable for rapid deployment and flexible enough for both peacekeeping missions and conventional combat. Meanwhile, the so-called revolution in military affairs (RMA) was incorporating more advanced communications and information management technology to battlefield use, in order to maintain American forces' technological edge.

BUDGET   The extended period of U.S. economic growth, coupled with budget surpluses in fiscal years 1998 and 1999 (US$69.2 billion and US$122.7 billion, respectively), facilitated another increase, albeit modest, in the U.S. defense budget, from US$265 billion for 1999 to US$268 billion for fiscal year 2000. Despite a drop of nearly 30 percent in real terms between 1985 and 1998, total U.S. defense spending in 1998 was five times that of Russia, whose spending was the second highest in Asia Pacific (see Overview, table 1). This level of spending is a major factor underlying American military superiority in the region.

ISSUES   After China, the United States has the second largest active duty armed forces in the world (see Overview, table 1). Nevertheless, the numbers of U.S. active duty military personnel declined over the 1990s, falling by some 35 percent to approximately 1.40 million in 1999. With American economic growth continually generating new private-sector jobs, the military has had difficulty meeting recruitment goals for the all-volunteer force. In fiscal year 1999, despite lowered qualification criteria and monetary incentives, recruitment for all services was 7 percent below target. Lengthy and repeated overseas deployments were also reported to be affecting retention of personnel in the navy and air force, especially skilled personnel such as pilots. These issues have led to concerns over readiness and "overstretch" in the armed forces.

Continuing issues in U.S. defense policy include differences in priorities between Congress and the executive branch over spending, particularly development and procurement of new weapons systems, which is important to the economies of many Congressional districts. For example, in 1999 Congress voted increases in spending on the F-22, a new air force fighter, and in the number of aircraft to be purchased despite questions in the executive branch about the plane's cost effectiveness. Base closings are another perennial issue between the legislative and executive branches, with Congress refusing to approve base closings that the Defense Department favors to save costs.

Thus, a key challenge for U.S. defense policy remains maintaining an appropriate balance between meeting current needs for manpower, equipment, and training, and investing in the development of new force structures and the acquisition of new weapons systems. An end to the long period of economic expansion would exacerbate budget issues generally, including defense spending and related policy questions.

Finally, increasing U.S. technological superiority and the ongoing RMA raise issues, both within the United States and among its allies, about managing America's alliance relationships. There are concerns over how to maintain interoperability and effective cooperation with allies, and over the future division of labor within the alliances. Technological change can also affect U.S. forward basing arrangements. The U.S. commitment of 100,000 forward based troops in Asia Pacific already involves delicate economic and political issues in Japan and Korea, as well as new concerns over terrorism and other threats to U.S. bases. Growing U.S. ability to project power from the United States may lead to increased questioning, both in the United States and the host countries, of the need to sustain the American forward presence at current levels.

CONTRIBUTIONS TO REGIONAL AND GLOBAL SECURITY

PEACEKEEPING   The dilemmas of defining post–cold war U.S. security policy were pointedly illustrated in the two major international interventions during 1999—Kosovo and East Timor—both of which continued into the year 2000.

The Clinton administration's handling of Kosovo was strongly influenced by its experience with Bosnia, where international inaction had prolonged the conflict and multiplied the human toll. Thus, faced with public outcry in the United States and mounting demands for international action against Serbian oppression of ethnic Albanians in Kosovo, the administration took a highly proactive stance. The United States orchestrated a concerted diplomatic effort to persuade and pressure Yugoslav President Slobodan Milosevic to agree to a negotiated autonomy arrangement. When that effort failed, in late March 1999 the United States took the lead in a two-and-a-half-month bombing campaign. Then, in June, following Serbian agreement to withdraw from Kosovo, the United States became one of four major troop contributors to the Kosovo Force (KFOR) peacekeeping operation.

The air campaign was chosen to minimize allied casualties. Its principal features were an initial focus on Serb air defenses and extensive reliance on high-technology weaponry. This resulted in several unexpected consequences. The campaign succeeded, but it took longer than anticipated, and it did not stop—and may even have accelerated—Serbian ethnic cleansing in Kosovo. Second, the more advanced U.S. aircraft had to fly a disproportionate share of sorties in a nominally multilateral effort, and American stocks of costly cruise missiles were nearly exhausted. Finally, the virtual absence of American casualties conveyed an image of overwhelming U.S. technological superiority, arousing concerns, including in Asia, about a "Kosovo syndrome"—i.e., increased U.S. interventionism. This perception was reinforced by President Clinton's statement in June that "Where we have the ability to do so, we . . . must take a stand" against efforts "to systematically destroy or displace an entire people." American media commentary dubbed this the "Clinton Doctrine."

The East Timor case was quite different. The United States played an active role, along with Australia, in the international effort to persuade the Indonesian government to stop the rampage by pro-Indonesian militias following the overwhelming vote for East Timor independence in the August 30 referendum. However, from the outset U.S. leaders virtually ruled out the use of American combat forces in any military intervention or peacekeeping operation. When Indonesia agreed to accept an international force in mid-September, direct U.S. participation was limited to logistical support and specialized personnel. (Nevertheless, U.S. support to INTERFET was more substantial than generally recognized. Second only to Australia in financial terms, it included the amphibious assault ship USS *Belleau Wood*, carrying elements of a Marine Expeditionary Unit with helicopters, landing craft, and other equipment. The *Belleau Wood* provided heavy helicopter transport and numerous other services, and could have landed ground troops.)

The rationale for not contributing a combat contingent to INTERFET boiled down to the arguments that other countries, such as Australia, were closer to East Timor and thus more directly affected, and that the American public and Congress were unlikely to support a U.S. combat role there. Underlying these arguments was awareness that U.S. strategic interests in East Timor were not widely recognized by the American public. This position invited criticism from both directions: from Indonesians and other Asians angry at Western interventionism, and from some Australians and others who saw the United States as unreliable and inconsistent in its response to massive human rights abuses.

One consistent feature in the U.S. approach in both Kosovo and Timor was determination to minimize American casualties. At the heart of the emerging U.S. policy on participation in international interventions seems to be the assumption that, unless critical U.S. interests are at stake, the American public and Congress will not accept commitments involving numerous or steady casualties. An additional consideration is the stress on the armed forces of multiple, simultaneous commitments.

These factors, combined with the wish to defuse perceptions of a "Kosovo syndrome," may have motivated President Clinton, in his address to the UN General Assembly in September, to restate the "Clinton Doctrine" in more qualified terms, emphasizing differences between specific situations and the danger of "promising too much."

ASIA PACIFIC SECURITY ARRANGEMENTS Other aspects of long-standing U.S. security relationships with Asia Pacific countries continue, and the levels of activity of these relationships are relatively intense. They include frequent exchanges of visits and consultations, regular bilateral and multilateral exercises, and the development of arrangements for greater access, such as to Singapore's new Changi Naval Base. One outstanding obstacle to such cooperation was cleared in 1999, when the Philippines Senate approved the Philippines-U.S. Visiting Forces Agreement, making possible the resumption of U.S. troop participation in joint exercises in the Philippines. Military cooperation with Indonesia was suspended due to the East Timor events, but with the advent of the Wahid government a resumption of this relationship appeared likely in 2000. The United States also continues to participate in multilateral regional organizations such as APEC and the ASEAN Regional Forum, and to pursue "minilateral" dialogues such as the U.S.-Japan-Korea Trilateral Coordination and Oversight Group on policy regarding North Korea.

GLOBAL SETBACKS: CTBT AND UN DUES Two actions by the U.S. Congress during 1999 could have longer-term impact on the U.S. contribution to international security. The first was the rejection of the Comprehensive Test Ban Treaty (CTBT) in October by the Republican majority in the U.S. Senate. The United States had played a major role in the negotiation of this treaty to counter nuclear proliferation and following the Indian and Pakistani nuclear tests in 1998 had pressed the two South Asian states very hard to accede to the treaty. But critics of the treaty in the Senate cited doubts over verification and the need for continued testing to maintain the U.S. nuclear deterrent. The Clinton administration pledged to continue to press for ratification and to maintain the voluntary moratorium on testing. However, defeat of the CTBT was generally seen as weakening the U.S. contribution to the high-priority antiproliferation effort.

The other global setback was refusal by Congress to approve full funding of outstanding U.S. dues to the United Nations. This raised the possibility that, as provided in the UN Charter, the United States might lose its vote in the leading international institution. The United States ultimately paid an amount sufficient to maintain its right to vote, but set conditions on any further back payments. This ensured that the U.S. conditions and the U.S. contribution to the United Nations would remain contentious issues for the foreseeable future, with uncertain impact on the standing of the United States in the United Nations as well as the effectiveness of the body itself.

18 Vietnam

The Security Environment

Vietnam entered the year 2000 with a basically stable security environment, as it worked actively toward greater integration into the Association of Southeast Asian Nations (ASEAN) and the wider Asia Pacific
regional community. However, at the same time, Vietnam faces serious
internal and external challenges. These range from the need to boost
economic growth and fight corruption and other social vices at home,
to the need to settle disputes with neighbors over maritime claims in the
adjacent South China Sea, to the danger of instability in neighboring
Southeast Asian countries affected by the 1997–1998 economic crisis,
particularly Indonesia.

Vietnam's leaders are also concerned over the impact, on the country and the region, of broader global trends such as tensions in relations
among major powers and the precedent of Western intervention in the
internal affairs of states over human rights issues, as exemplified by the
Kosovo war. Fundamentally, the Vietnamese government recognizes that
in the face of increasing globalization, there is no practical alternative
to integration into the world community, but that the downside of globalization is greater volatility and internal vulnerability.

INTERNAL   Since 1994, Vietnam has identified two principal internal
threats to its national security: the danger of lagging behind other countries economically, a threat that becomes more acute, and with larger
consequence, in the highly competitive global environment; and problems such as bureaucratization, corruption, and social vices that could
damage unity, stability, and the social order.

178

To deal with the first threat, the Vietnamese government accelerated its economic reform process. During 1990–1996, the average annual gross domestic product growth rate was 8.5 percent. Vietnam's economy was severely affected by the 1997–1998 Asian financial crisis, and it experienced sharp declines in exports and inflows of foreign investment, higher unemployment, and slower growth. Its growth rate in 1997 fell to 8.2 percent, in 1998 to 5.8 percent, and in 1999 to an estimated 4–5 percent. Vietnamese policymakers are concerned that, while other Asian economies are recovering, Vietnam's downturn continues.

In 1997 and 1998, the government adopted a range of measures to reverse the downturn. These included, in particular, mobilizing domestic economic development as well as promoting international integration; enhancing the efficiency and competitiveness of the economy; expediting agricultural development to keep pace with modernization; putting domestic and foreign investment to effective use; increasing the efficiency of state-owned enterprises; and reforming the financial and banking system.

In 1999, further measures were implemented to get the economy back on track:

- Accelerating Official Development Assistance (ODA) disbursement and mobilizing an additional VND7,400 billion (US$527 million at US$1 = VND14,041) of domestic capital for investment;
- Increasing lending to the agricultural processing industry for development of rural infrastructure;
- Expanding the search for new export markets through an Export Support Fund;
- Accelerating corporatization of state-owned enterprises and creating equal conditions for all types of business; and
- Increasing funding for poverty reduction and development of the social safety net and insurance system.

Social safety and order have largely been maintained, but widespread corruption has become a serious concern. In some rural areas, there have been public protests against corrupt officials. The government has instituted strong measures to punish corruption and promote administrative reform. The Communist Party of Vietnam has also announced a two-year reorganization campaign to raise the quality of party members and officials and thereby enhance the party's image in the society.

EXTERNAL   The world community faces challenges arising from ethnic tensions and conflicts, military intervention in the internal affairs of a country, and the gap between richer and poorer countries, among other economic and political problems. Despite these developments, however, the basic trend of peace, stability, and cooperation for development prevails at the global and regional levels.

The most significant international event of 1999 was the three-month war in Yugoslavia launched by the North Atlantic Treaty Organization (NATO) in March. Although the war was limited in time (seventy-nine days), scale (only air force and missiles were used), and space (Yugoslavian territory), it had tremendous impact on the global security environment and Asia Pacific's no less. First, countries in Asia Pacific had differing attitudes toward the war, and this affected the regional confidence-building process. Second, the war was a watershed, as Western countries placed human rights above national sovereignty and challenged the basic principle of noninterference in a country's internal affairs. With countries in the region facing ethnic tension and social instability arising from the economic crisis, this emphasis in U.S. and Western policy is cause for concern. Third, the war has affected the position and role of the major world powers and the relations among them. The U.S. bombing of the Chinese embassy in Belgrade damaged Sino-U.S relations and therefore upset the security environment of Asia Pacific. Fourth, the demonstration of military technological advances in the Kosovo war may spark an arms race, which could disrupt the regional process of confidence building and divert attention and resources from overcoming the economic crisis. Vietnam nevertheless believes that a similar war in Asia is unlikely, as the situation in Asia is considerably different from that of Europe.

While struggling to overcome the consequences of the economic crisis, countries in Asia Pacific also face the continuing challenge of managing the impact of globalization. For a long time, it seemed that globalization would bring benefit to all. Since the economic crisis, analysts and policymakers, including some in Vietnam, have begun to consider seriously the costs of globalization as well. These include the likelihood of more frequent currency and financial crises, increased income inequality within and among countries, disruption of social cohesion, and limits on a government's policy choices. However, this has not led countries to turn toward policies of isolation or insulation. Instead, almost all countries continue to prepare themselves for integration into the world economy.

East Asian countries have been implementing reform measures in order to recover from the economic crisis. There are encouraging signs of recovery, as most of the affected countries have been able to restore the confidence of domestic and foreign investors. Economic growth rates in 1999 were positive and in many cases better than originally expected. Experts agree, however, that the region's fundamental problems are deeper, wider, and potentially more destabilizing than had previously been realized. Growing unemployment, ethnic tensions, and social and political instability have become the highest priority problems of many countries in the region.

Indonesia is the most critical case. Despite the beginnings of economic recovery and successful parliamentary and presidential elections in 1999, the prospects for political and social stability remain extremely uncertain. In addition, the East Timor situation and secessionist movements in other Indonesian regions affect the region's security environment. Given Indonesia's large population, strategic location, and significant role in ASEAN, a deterioration of Indonesia's stability would be a source of serious concern for the region.

Vietnam believes that the state of relations among the United States, China, and Japan is also important for peace, stability, and development in Asia Pacific. As of 1998, all three countries appeared to be constructing viable frameworks for their bilateral relations in the twenty-first century. However, developments in 1999 showed that a whole range of issues can disrupt these relations if they are not properly managed. For Sino-American relations, there are issues of human rights, trade (including China's entry into the World Trade Organization, Taiwan, missile defense, and the bombing of the Chinese embassy in Belgrade. For Sino-Japanese relations, there are issues concerning history, the interpretation of the new Guidelines for U.S.-Japan Defense Cooperation, and territorial disputes. The deterioration of U.S.-China relations, though somewhat recovered toward the end of 1999, also affected U.S. and Chinese relations with other countries as well as the overall security environment of the region.

Territorial disputes in the South China Sea are another focus of concern for Asia Pacific. Developments in 1999 included China's unilateral ban on fishing for three months in the South China Sea, and Malaysia's construction of facilities on two islets in the disputed Spratly Islands. These activities were not consistent with the 1992 ASEAN declaration on the South China Sea and further complicated the problems.

DEFENSE POLICIES AND ISSUES

DEFENSE DOCTRINE   Vietnam's defense doctrine consists of three main elements:
- Prevention of war and the threat of war;
- Participation of the entire population, not just the armed forces, in protecting the country; and
- Comprehensive national strength—economic, political, cultural, military, and diplomatic.

The national defense policy based on this doctrine was set out in Vietnam's first white paper, released in 1998, entitled "Vietnam—Consolidating National Defense, Safeguarding the Homeland." The terms of this policy, which remains in effect, specify peace and self-defense as basic national principles; the importance of national interests, independence, sovereignty, and territorial integrity; the prevention and punishment of crime; social order and safety; open, diverse, and multilateral external relations; opposition to aggression and the proliferation of weapons of mass destruction; noninterference in internal affairs of nations; and peaceful resolution of disputes.

BUILDING THE PEOPLE'S ARMY   Vietnam is engaged in restructuring and renewing its armed forces, and has made considerable progress toward this end.

First of all, Vietnam sees its national security in the framework of regional security and global security. Therefore, Vietnam seeks progressive integration into the regional and world community and cooperation with other countries for mutual security and development. At the same time, as regards the two strategic tasks of national construction and national defense, Vietnam accords priority to the former. This choice greatly affects Vietnam's approach to developing its armed forces.

Second, the Vietnamese government has decided to reduce the size of its active military by two-thirds, even as it builds up its reserves, militia, and self-defense forces. This military reduction has created a new balance among the three branches. Within the regular forces, emphasis is placed on improving quality and combat capability.

Third, acquisition of weapons and technology will proceed gradually, in conformity with Vietnam's capacities. In selecting weaponry, the main criteria are maintenance (self-reliance), durability (resilience), economy, and quality improvement.

CONTRIBUTIONS TO REGIONAL AND GLOBAL SECURITY

The government of Vietnam has been making major efforts to strengthen its bilateral relations, especially with neighboring countries. It considers these efforts as positive contributions to both Vietnam's own security environment and the peace and stability of the region.

Vietnam attaches great importance to stable relations with its giant neighbor China. In February 1999, during a visit to China by Communist Party General Secretary Le Kha Phieu, the two countries agreed to strengthen their bilateral relationship on the basis of the following principles: "Friendly Neighbors, Long-term Stability, Looking to the Future." They reaffirmed their commitment to complete negotiations for a land border agreement in 1999 and an agreement on border delineation in the Gulf of Tonkin in the year 2000. The countries also agreed not to take any action that would exacerbate the dispute over territorial claims in the South China Sea, and to negotiate a long-term solution to the issue. The Land Border Treaty was signed on December 30, an important event in Vietnam-China relations.

Vietnam-Cambodia relations have entered a new era, as both countries are now members of ASEAN and have adhered to principles in the ASEAN Treaty of Amity and Cooperation governing relationships among member countries. The year 1999 was marked by an increased exchange of high-level visits. In May and July, the leaders of Cambodia's National Assembly and Senate visited Vietnam. In June, the general secretary of Vietnam's Communist Party visited Cambodia. As a result of these visits, the two countries reached agreement on the following formula to guide their bilateral relationship: "Good Neighborly Cooperation, Traditional Friendly Solidarity, Long-term Stability." They also agreed to conclude a border demarcation agreement in the year 2000.

Traditional friendly relations between Vietnam and Laos were strengthened by the visit of Vietnam's President Tran Duc Luong to Laos in June 1999. The two sides discussed mutual cooperation in overcoming the difficulties caused by the economic crisis and in effectively integrating into the region.

Vietnam's bilateral relations with the major powers, particularly with Japan, are being consolidated. During a visit by Vietnam's Prime Minister Phan Van Khai to Japan in March, the two sides agreed to grant each other long-term "most-favored nation" trading status, and to increase economic, cultural, and political cooperation. They also agreed to begin military dialogues and exchanges. In October, Vietnam hosted the first ASEAN-Japan Vision 2020 consultation meeting, aimed at identifying means to improve ASEAN-Japan relations in the twenty-first century.

As part of the process of integration into the region and the world, Vietnam is progressively taking a more active role in multilateral institutions and processes. Vietnam organized the official ceremony to admit Cambodia into ASEAN in April, fulfilling the ASEAN founders' dream of an ASEAN-10. Vietnam then hosted a conference of ASEAN financial ministers to discuss ways of implementing the Hanoi Plan of Action—agreed upon at the 6th ASEAN Summit held December 1998 in Hanoi—on macroeconomic policy coordination, particularly financial issues.

The ASEAN Regional Forum (ARF) is the only regional multilateral mechanism for discussing security issues and confidence building among the participating countries. Vietnam is working actively with other members to strengthen the ARF process. For example, Vietnam and the Philippines are jointly drafting a Code of Conduct in the South China Sea. Meanwhile, the Vietnamese government encourages think tanks to participate in and contribute to regional nongovernmental track two organizations such as the Council for Security Cooperation in Asia Pacific (CSCAP), the ASEAN Institutes for Strategic and International Studies network, and the Eastern Hemisphere Research Institutes network, which complement the governmental track one activities in the ARF and other forums.

As one of the newest members of the Asia-Pacific Economic Cooperation (APEC) forum, Vietnam is preparing its own voluntary action plan to implement the APEC objectives of trade and investment liberalization and facilitation in Asia Pacific. At the same time, Vietnam is working to fulfill its obligations under the ASEAN Free Trade Area and the ASEAN Investment Area, and especially to implement the Hanoi Plan of Action.

At the global level, Vietnam has shown its willingness to take a more active role at the United Nations, especially in the functional organizations such as the Economic and Social Council (ECOSOC), of which Vietnam is a member for the 1998–2000 term. Vietnam is also cooperating in the effort to reform the United Nations, particularly the Security Council, to conform with changing global conditions.

List of Abbreviations

ABM   Anti-Ballistic Missile (Treaty)
ABRI   Angkatan Bersenjata Republik Indonesia (Indonesian Armed Forces)
ACSA   Acquisition and Cross-Servicing Agreement (Japan-United States)
ADF   Australian Defense Force
AFP   Armed Forces of the Philippines
ANKI   Independent Khmer National Army
ANZUS   Australia-New Zealand-United States defense alliance
APEC   Asia-Pacific Economic Cooperation
ARATS   Association for Relations Across the Taiwan Strait
ARF   ASEAN Regional Forum
ARMM   Autonomous Region in Muslim Mindanao (Philippines)
ASEAN   Association of Southeast Asian Nations
ASEM   Asia-Europe Meeting
ATACMS   army tactical missile system
BIMSTEC   Bangladesh-India-Myanmar-Sri Lanka-Thailand Economic Cooperation
BJP   Bharatiya Janata Party (Indian People's Party)
BPC   Bougainville People's Congress (PNG)
BRA   Bougainville Revolutionary Army (PNG)
CARAT-V/99   Cooperation Afloat Readiness and Training (Indonesia-United States)
CGDK   Coalition Government of Democratic Kampuchea
CIS   Commonwealth of Independent States
CLOB   Central Limit Order Book (Singapore)
CMC   Central Military Commission (China)
CPP   Cambodian People's Party

CSCAP   Council for Security Cooperation in Asia Pacific
CST   (Tashkent) Collective Security Treaty (CIS)
CTBT   Comprehensive Test Ban Treaty
CTR   Cooperative Threat Reduction (program, Russia-United States)
DPR   Dewan Perwakilan Rakyat (national parliament of Indonesia)
DSO   Defense Science Organization (Singapore)
DSTA   Defense Science and Technology Agency (Singapore)
DTG   Defense Technology Group (Singapore)
ECOSOC   Economic and Social Council
EEZ   Exclusive Economic Zone
Ealaf   East-Asia Latin American Forum
FPDA   Five Power Defense Arrangements (Australia, Malaysia, New Zealand, Singapore, and the United Kingdom)
G-8   Group of Eight
GAM   Gerakan Aceh Merdeka (Free Aceh Movement, Indonesia)
GMS   Greater Mekong Subregion
GUUAM   Georgia, Ukraine, Uzbekistan, Azerbaijan, and Moldova
ICBM   intercontinental ballistic missile
ILO   International Labor Organization
IMF   International Monetary Fund
INF   Intermediate-Range Nuclear Forces
INTERFET   International Force in East Timor
IOR-ARC   Indian Ocean Rim Association for Regional Cooperation
ISG   Inter-sessional Support Group (ARF)
ISO   internal security operations (Philippines)
JCC   (ASEAN-European Commission) Joint Cooperation Committee
JDA   Japan Defense Agency
KEDO   Korean Peninsula Energy Development Organization
KFOR   Kosovo Force
KMT   Nationalist Party (Taiwan)
LDP   Liberal Democratic Party (Japan)
MILF   Moro Islamic Liberation Front (Philippines)
MLRS   multiple launch rocket system
MNLF   Moro National Liberation Front (Philippines)
MOU   memorandum of understanding
MPR   Majelis Permusyawaratan Rakyat (People's Consultative Assembly, of Indonesia)
MRF   multirole fighter
MSDF   Maritime Self-Defense Force (Japan)
MTCR   Missile Technology Control Regime

NATO   North Atlantic Treaty Organization
NDF   National Democratic Front (Philippines)
NMD   national missile defense
NPA   New People's Army (Philippines)
NPT   Nonproliferation Treaty
NTWD   Navy Theater Wide Defense (Japan-United States)
NZDF   New Zealand Defense Force
ODA   Official Development Assistance
OPM   Organisasi Papua Merdeka (Free Papua Movement)
OPV   offshore patrol vessels
OSCE   Organization for Security and Cooperation in Europe
PCTNC   Philippine Center on Transnational Crime
PECC   Pacific Economic Cooperation Council
PLA   People's Liberation Army (China)
PNG   Papua New Guinea
PNGDF   Papua New Guinea Defense Force
PNP   Philippine National Police
PPKB   Brunei National Solidarity Party
PRB   Brunei Peoples' Party
PRC   People's Republic of China
PRK   People's Republic of Kampuchea
RCAF   Royal Cambodian Armed Forces
RMA   "revolution in military affairs"
RSAF   Republic of Singapore Air Force
RSN   Republic of Singapore Navy
SAARC   South Asian Association for Regional Cooperation
SADC   Southern Africa Development Community
SAF   Singapore Armed Forces
SAM   surface-to-air missile
SDF   Self-Defense Forces (Japan)
SFOR   Stabilization Force (Bosnia)
SLBM   submarine-launched ballistic missile
SSOD IV   Fourth Special Session of the UN General Assembly Devoted
   to Disarmament
START   Strategic Arms Reduction Treaty
TCOG   Trilateral Coordination and Oversight Group (United States-
   Japan-South Korea)
TMD   theater missile defense
TNI   Tentara Nasional Indonesia (Indonesian National Military)
UNDC   UN Disarmament Commission

UNHCHR   UN High Commissioner for Human Rights
UNHCR   UN High Commisioner for Refugees
UNIFIL   UN Interim Force in Lebanon
UNSCOM   UN Special Commission (in Iraq)
UNTAET   UN Transitional Administration in East Timor
UNTSO   UN Truce Supervision Organization (Jerusalem)
UWSA   (Burmese Wa's) United Wa State Army
WMD   weapons of mass destruction
WTO   World Trade Organization

The APSO Project Team

A distinctive feature of the *Asia Pacific Security Outlook* is that it is based on background papers developed by analysts from the region. These analysts, many of them younger specialists, meet at an annual workshop to examine each country paper and discuss the overall regional outlook. They also complete a questionnaire on regional security issues, which is used to develop the regional overview and provide an assessment of changing perceptions over time.

Those involved in the process of developing the 2000 *Asia Pacific Security Outlook* include the following people. (Note: Paper writers participated in their individual capacities; their views do not necessarily represent those of the institutions with which they are affiliated.)

COUNTRY ANALYSTS
(BACKGROUND PAPER WRITER IDENTIFIED BY AN ASTERISK)

AUSTRALIA   Ross Cottrill, Australian Institute of International Affairs*

BRUNEI DARUSSALAM   Pushpa Thambipillai, University of Brunei Darussalam*

CAMBODIA   Kao Kim Hourn, Cambodian Institute for Cooperation and Peace*

CANADA   Brian L. Job, University of British Columbia*

CHINA   Chu Shulong, China Institute of Contemporary International Relations*

EUROPEAN UNION   Hanns Maull, University of Trier*

INDIA   Dipankar Banerjee, Regional Centre for Strategic Studies,* Colombo

INDONESIA   Rizal Sukma, Centre for Strategic and International Studies*

JAPAN   Murata Kōji, Hiroshima University*
REPUBLIC OF KOREA   Oknim Chung, Sejong Institute*
NEW ZEALAND   David Dickens, Victoria University of Wellington*
PAPUA NEW GUIDEA   Ronald J. May, Australian National University*; Dorke Gedare, Papua New Guinea National Research Institute
PHILIPPINES   Raymund Jose Quilop, Institute for Strategic and Development Studies*
RUSSIA   Dmitri V. Trenin, Carnegie Moscow Center, Carnegie Endowment for International Peace*
SINGAPORE   Lam Peng Er, National University of Singapore*
THAILAND   Julaporn Euarukskul, Thammasat University*
UNITED STATES   Richard W. Baker, East-West Center*
VIETNAM   Bui Thanh Son, Institute of International Relations*

OVERVIEW

Charles E. Morrison, President, East-West Center

EDITORS

Richard W. Baker, International Relations Specialist, East-West Center
Charles E. Morrison, President, East-West Center

PROJECT DIRECTORS

Charles E. Morrison, President, East-West Center (United States)
Nishihara Masashi, Professor of International Relations, National Defense Academy (Japan)
Jusuf Wanandi, Chairman of the Supervisory Board, Center for Strategic and International Studies (Indonesia)

STAFF SUPPORT

Furuya Ryōta, Assistant Program Officer, Japan Center for International Exchange
Kawaguchi Chie, Assistant Editor, Japan Center for International Exchange
Nio Chikako, Program Associate, Japan Center for International Exchange
Sumoge Takako, Assistant Program Officer, Japan Center for International Exchange

Index

Asia Pacific Agenda Project

The Asia Pacific Agenda Project (APAP) was established in November 1995 to enhance policy-oriented intellectual exchange at the nongovernmental level, with special emphasis on independent research institutions in the region. It consists of four interconnected components: (1) the Asia Pacific Agenda Forum, a gathering of leaders of Asia Pacific policy research institutes to explore the future agenda for collaborative research and dialogue activities related to the development of an Asia Pacific community; (2) an Asia Pacific policy research information network utilizing the Internet; (3) annual multilateral joint research projects on pertinent issues of regional and global importance undertaken in collaboration with major research institutions in the region; and (4) collaborative research activities designed to nurture a new generation of Asia Pacific leaders who can participate in international intellectual dialogues. APAP is managed by an international steering committee composed of nine major research institutions in the region. The Japan Center for International Exchange has served as secretariat since APAP's inception.

ASEAN Institutes for Strategic and International Studies

ASEAN-ISIS (Institutes for Strategic and International Studies) is an association of nongovernmental organizations registered with the Association of Southeast Asian Nations. Formed in 1988, its membership comprises the Centre for Strategic and International Studies (CSIS) of Indonesia, the Institute of Strategic and International Studies (ISIS) of Malaysia, the Institute for Strategic and Development Studies (ISDS) of the Philippines, the Singapore Institute of International Affairs (SIIA), and the Institute of Security and International Studies (ISIS) of Thailand. Its purpose is to encourage cooperation and coordination of activities among policy-oriented ASEAN scholars and analysts, and to promote policy-oriented studies of, and exchange of information and viewpoints on, various strategic and international issues affecting Southeast Asia's and ASEAN's peace, security, and well-being.

East-West Center

Established by the United States Congress in 1960 to promote mutual understanding and cooperation among the governments and peoples of the Asia Pacific region, including the United States, the East-West Center seeks to foster the development of an Asia Pacific community through cooperative study, training, and research. Center activities focus on the promotion of shared regional values and the building of regional institutions and arrangements; the promotion of economic growth with equity, stability, and sustainability; and the management and resolution of critical regional as well as common problems.

Japan Center for International Exchange

Founded in 1970, the Japan Center for International Exchange (JCIE) is an independent, nonprofit, and nonpartisan organization dedicated to strengthening Japan's role in international affairs. JCIE believes that Japan faces a major challenge in augmenting its positive contributions to the international community, in keeping with its position as one of the world's largest industrial democracies. Operating in a country where policy making has traditionally been dominated by the government bureaucracy, JCIE has played an important role in broadening debate on Japan's international responsibilities by conducting international and cross-sectional programs of exchange, research, and discussion.

JCIE creates opportunities for informed policy discussions; it does not take policy positions. JCIE programs are carried out with the collaboration and cosponsorship of many organizations. The contacts developed through these working relationships are crucial to JCIE's efforts to increase the number of Japanese from the private sector engaged in meaningful policy research and dialogue with overseas counterparts. JCIE receives no government subsidies; rather, funding comes from private foundation grants, corporate contributions, and contracts.